THE BETTER-THAN-TAKEOUT
# Thai Cookbook

# THE BETTER-THAN-TAKEOUT Thai COOKBOOK

FAVORITE THAI FOOD RECIPES
MADE AT HOME

Danette St. Onge

ROCKRIDGE
PRESS

Cover photography © Hélène Dujardin
Back cover photography © Paritha Wannawanit; Trent Lanz/Stocksy
Interior photography © Jill Chen/Stocksy, p.ii; Paritha Wannawanit, p.v; Dorota Indycka/Stockfood, p.xii; Trent Lanz/Stocksy, p.28; Jill Chen/Stocksy, p.30; Lena Mirisola/Getty, p.50; Tina Bumann/Stockfood, p.88; Sangdad Media Group/Stockfood, p.118; Jill Chen/Stocksy, p.121; Paritha Wannawanit, p.156; Paritha Wannawanit, p.168; Paritha Wannawanit, p.182; Paritha Wannawanit, p.202; Paritha Wannawanit, p.216; Paritha Wannawanit, p.224; Mick Shippen/Stockfood, p.228; Paritha Wannawanit, p.244
Author photo © Steve Babuljak

ISBN: Print 978-1-62315-861-3 | eBook 978-1-62315-862-0

To my mother, Patawin, who taught me that
making and sharing good food
is an expression of love.

# Contents

# Introduction

With its delicate balance of five flavors—sweet, sour, salty, bitter, and spicy—Thai food has become a restaurant favorite since it was introduced to American diners in the 1960s and '70s. In some cities, it's now a more popular takeout option than pizza. There's nothing more comforting after a long day of work than ordering Thai food and curling up on the couch in front of the TV. But with just a bit of preparation and effort—and not much more time than it takes to drive to your local takeout joint for pickup or wait for the delivery guy—those same satisfying, tasty dishes can be made at home.

Cooking at home is cheaper and healthier than takeout—you can use fresh, high-quality ingredients and control the amounts of oil, salt, and sugar. In addition, you have precise control over spice levels, rather than trusting in nonstandardized restaurant "spiciness" scales and hoping for the best. You can also make just one dish and customize each serving for individual tastes in your household, rather than having to call in separate orders for those who can't get enough chile heat and those who prefer their flavors mild.

Another—perhaps surprising—argument for making your own Thai food is the fact that, in many places, this is the only way to get more authentic Thai tastes. To cater to palates that have been trained by the prevalence of Chinese American restaurants, Thai restaurants in the United States often feature dishes that are not actually Thai at all, or that have been so Westernized that they would not be considered authentic by purists.

By offering "pick-your-protein" and "pick-your-spice-level" menus, American Thai eateries have, perhaps unwittingly, made it so that even avid Thai-food devotees might be unfamiliar with how these dishes are usually made in Thailand, and they lose that all-important balance between the five flavors. Plus, many of the simple-yet-satisfying favorites that Thai people make regularly at home are rarely found on Thai takeout menus. Even with the constraint of limited access to Asian ingredients, making your own Thai food can get you much closer to the "real deal."

Probably the number-one deterrent to attempting Thai cuisine at home is the perception, due to its complex, layered flavors, that it is very complicated and labor intensive. While some specialties, such as delicacies originally intended for the Thai royal court, do require hard-to-find ingredients or are laborious to prepare, many just-as-traditional Thai dishes are neither difficult nor time consuming and can easily be made at home with ingredients available in most markets, no special equipment required. These dishes will be our focus in this book.

As for my own experience with Thai cuisine, it's quite an East-West fusion itself. I was born in California to a Thai mother and an American father. My mother was a skilled cook, famous among her friends for not only her Thai and Chinese cooking but her American, European, and Middle Eastern dishes as well. She instilled a love of food and cooking in me from a young age, and we cooked and ate together often, from stir-fries and curries to baking cakes and making coq au vin, often followed by Thai noodle soup for a midnight snack.

When I was 10, my family moved to Bangkok and we lived there for several years. It was during this time that I became really familiar with the Thai way of eating, from breakfast through that midnight snack and all the many meals and snack breaks in between (I think perhaps the only beings that eat more often than Thais are Hobbits).

After our return to California, my family opened a Thai restaurant, where I assisted my mother in ordering ingredients, devising the menu, and serving customers. Through this experience, I learned which Thai dishes are most popular with American customers and how to adapt traditional Thai food in the context of available ingredients and prevailing tastes.

This book will walk you through navigating Asian markets and stocking your pantry and kitchen for Thai cooking, as well as explain common Thai cooking techniques. The quick-and-easy recipes include iconic dishes from Thai restaurant menus, homey family favorites, and street-food classics. Along with helpful tips and shortcuts, and suggestions for substitutions when necessary, it gives you all you need to become an adept Thai cook. Once you've got the hang of it, you might never reach for a takeout menu again!

# CHAPTER ONE

# The Thai Kitchen

The key to having a delicious Thai meal on your table in an hour or less is preparation. That means having your kitchen stocked with a few essential Thai ingredients and some basic equipment, organizing everything, and timing tasks just right. Most of the foods, condiments, and equipment you'll need can be found at major supermarkets and Asian grocery stores, but other options include local farmers' markets and online shops (see Resources, page 250). Many of the sauces and pastes can be made ahead of time and kept on hand for weeks or months, so that you can easily make a favorite curry or noodle dish in less than half an hour.

Once you have the staples on hand and get the hang of a few simple Thai cooking techniques, you'll be able to whip up countless Thai dishes at a moment's notice. Start by picking just one or two of your favorite Thai dishes, determine what ingredients you will need for those, and go from there. And don't get too caught up in worries about authenticity—while it is certainly important, Thai recipes vary from cook to cook, household to household, and between regions, so it would be difficult to say that there is only one "correct" way of making any Thai dish. Make them your own! Feel free to omit ingredients you don't like or can't find, add things you do like, or make use of the many substitutes or adjustments suggested in this chapter and in the recipes themselves.

# The Beauty of Balance

Thai cuisine is perhaps best known for its bold, fiery spice, but in fact its true defining characteristic is that of balance—specifically, a harmonious balance of five main flavors: sweet, salty, sour, bitter, and spicy. The key is to balance these flavors in each meal, whether within a single dish or by balancing flavors among several dishes—one of the reasons why Thai meals are served "family style," with several dishes (often a soup or curry, salad, and a stir-fry dish) eaten at the same time, together with rice. One dish might be quite spicy, one might be sour, another salty, another a bit sweet. There is also a balance of textures and temperatures—rarely is a Thai dish all one texture, without contrasting softness, crunch, and chew. Crisp, cool cucumber or bean sprouts are often added to dishes just before serving, but they're not there just as a pretty garnish—they act as the perfect counterbalance to steaming-hot fried rice or chewy noodles. Thai cuisine itself is a blend of many neighboring influences, including Indian, Chinese, Laotian, Burmese, and Malaysian, as well as Middle Eastern and European elements. This masterful blending and balance are what make Thai cuisine so unique.

Most Thai cooks don't follow recipes but let their taste buds be their guide, tasting and adjusting as they cook. In fact, I never saw my Thai mother follow a recipe unless she was making a foreign dish, such as cheesecake. Since heat levels can vary widely among a single batch of chiles, and limes might vary in sweetness or acidity according to source and season, relying simply on numbers and weight or volume measurements can never give exactly the same results every time. For the purposes of this book, and to aid those unfamiliar with the desired results, precise measurements are provided for every recipe. But as you gain experience and confidence, eventually you will reach the point where you no longer need to measure but will let your taste and intuition be your guide in achieving that all-important balance.

# The Basic Thai Pantry: Essential Ingredients

You'll find most of these essential items at any well-stocked Asian grocery store, or sometimes even in the international foods aisle of your local supermarket. Most are also available online (see Resources, page 250). I provided the Thai names and Thai script so that even if you can't read the characters, you can compare them to the label to confirm that you are buying the right thing. Whole dried spices are preferable to ground because they have more flavor and last longer.

## GRAINS/STAPLES

### RICE (KHAO, ข้าว)

Rice is so important to the Thai diet that the words for "rice" and "food" are one and the same. A common greeting is "Kin khao re yung?" meaning literally, "Have you eaten rice yet?" but with the intended meaning of "Have you eaten?" or even just "How are you?"

Many varieties of rice exist in Thailand, but aromatic, long-grain **jasmine rice** (khao hom mali, ข้าวหอมมะลิ) is the most prized and the most versatile type to keep on hand. It's not made or flavored with jasmine but has pearly white grains and a fragrance reminiscent of pandan leaf. Look for rice from Thailand labeled "jasmine," "hom mali," "fragrant," or "scented." A round, green-and-yellow seal that reads "Thai Hom Mali Rice" from the Thai Department of Foreign Trade is an indicator of quality. Golden Phoenix and Three Ladies are good brands to look for. While jasmine rice might be available in your supermarket, it will be much cheaper, fresher, and often of higher quality at an Asian market. "New crop" jasmine rice is softer, with a higher moisture content; use a bit less water when cooking it. It is a good choice for accompanying meals, but not as good for making fried rice, when drier rice is better.

Glutinous rice, or **sticky rice** (khao niew, ข้าวเหนียว), is used chiefly as the accompaniment for dishes from Northeastern Thailand (Isaan) and for desserts like Mango with Sweet Coconut Sticky Rice (page 223). Look for Thai brands such as Golden Phoenix and Three Ladies; they are sometimes labeled "glutinous rice" or "sweet rice."

STORAGE: In a cool, dry, dark place, where it will keep indefinitely.

SUBSTITUTES: In a pinch, basmati rice, or any other aromatic long-grain rice, is the closest approximation for jasmine rice, though it does not have the same taste or texture. Other types of sticky rice (Chinese and Japanese) are not equivalents of Thai sticky rice.

## NOODLES (GUAY TIAO, ก๋วยเตี๋ยว)

Noodles are second only to rice as a Thai staple, and many different types are used, including dried rice noodles in varying thicknesses (wide, thin, and vermicelli); fresh, flat rice noodles (wide and thin); bean thread, glass, or cellophane noodles (woon sen, วุ้นเส้น, made from mung beans); fresh, thin rice noodles (khanom jeen, ขนมจีน); and thin, fresh egg noodles (bamee, บะหมี่).

STORAGE: Dried noodles keep indefinitely in a cool, dry place, while fresh noodles must be refrigerated and used within a few days.

SUBSTITUTES: Dried noodles can be substituted for fresh in a pinch. Because fresh khanom jeen are nearly impossible to find outside Thailand, Japanese somen (thin, dried wheat noodles) are a good substitute. Dried khanom jeen are also sometimes sold in Asian markets, particularly those specializing in Thai ingredients.

## SAUCES, SEASONINGS, AND DRY SPICES

### COCONUT MILK (GATI, กะทิ)

Another staple, coconut milk, made by mixing grated coconut meat with water and then straining the liquid, is an important ingredient in most Thai curries and many desserts, soups, and other dishes. It's available frozen (preferable), canned, or in UHT form in Tetra Pak boxes. Brands to look for include Mae Ploy, Aroy-D, and Chaokoh, but check the ingredients to make sure that no sweeteners, guar gum, or any other emulsifiers or thickeners have been added. When making a curry, be sure to buy the kind for savory cooking rather than the kind intended for making desserts (usually the photo on the label will be a clue as to which type it is), which will not "crack." Tip: Before purchasing, give the can a shake to find a brand that has the least "sloshing," indicating that it contains the most coconut cream. However, never shake a can just before using it to make a curry, as you want to use the cream that has risen to the top (see "Cracking Coconut Milk," page 23).

THE BETTER-THAN-TAKEOUT Thai Cookbook

STORAGE: In the refrigerator for a few days, or it can be frozen for several months.

SUBSTITUTES: Avoid "light" versions, because the rich coconut cream that rises to the top is essential to making a successful curry. Coconut milk intended for drinking (or as a dairy substitute) will not work for Thai cooking. "Coconut cream" is the thicker cream that rises to the top (much like the cream that rises to the top of milk)–it can be bought separately or skimmed from the top of a can of coconut milk. Avoid "cream of coconut," which is sweetened.

## CURRY PASTE (NAM PRIK GAENG, น้ำพริกแกง)

These moist, thick pastes are made by grinding together an assortment of intensely flavored herbs and spices and are the basis for many Thai curries.

There is no shame in using store-bought curry paste as a substitute for freshly made, particularly if you cannot find the raw ingredients for making paste or just don't have the time. It's preferable to use a store-bought paste than to make your own with the wrong ingredients or without key ingredients. Many Thais use purchased curry paste when cooking at home, just as many Italians use canned or jarred tomatoes for convenience, or outside of peak tomato season. That said, brands that come in plastic tubs or plastic bags generally taste fresher and have a better texture than canned curry pastes. Mae Ploy is a good brand to look for.

STORAGE: Once opened, curry paste in a sealed plastic tub will keep in the refrigerator for several weeks and in the freezer for many months. The same is true for fresh, homemade curry pastes.

## FISH SAUCE (NAM PLA, น้ำปลา)

Fish sauce, a thin, clear-brown liquid made from fermented anchovies and very close to the prized garum used in Ancient Roman cuisine, is truly indispensable for Thai cooking. Despite its name and pungent scent, it does not have a "fishy" taste when cooked but is used to add saltiness, tang, and umami-packed complexity to any number of dishes. It can be found in most supermarkets, though Thai brands sold at Asian markets (such as Tra Chang, Mae Noy, or Tiparos) will generally be higher quality and much cheaper.

STORAGE: Refrigerated, it will last for many months. Opened bottles of fish sauce stored at room temperature will not go bad but will gradually evaporate and grow more concentrated.

SUBSTITUTES: There is no real substitute, though kosher and vegetarian versions are available for purchase, and recipes for homemade vegetarian or vegan versions, many made with dried mushrooms and diluted soy sauce, can be found online. Another vegetarian option is to just use salt instead, though the results will taste distinctly less "Thai." Still, it's preferable to just use salt in place of fish sauce rather than soy sauce or another sauce with a completely different flavor, unless the recipe already calls for soy sauce, in which case, simply omit the fish sauce and increase the amount of soy sauce.

## OYSTER SAUCE (NAM MUN HOY, น้ำมันหอย)

This thick and flavorful dark brown sauce is often used in stir-fries. Look for one made with real oyster extract, rather than an "oyster-flavored" sauce. Thai brands, such as Maekrua (แม่ครัว), tend to have richer flavor and less salt than Chinese brands.

STORAGE: Once opened, it will keep for up to one year in the refrigerator.

SUBSTITUTES: If you can't find oyster sauce, you can approximate your own by mixing a little fish sauce with hoisin sauce in a 1:5 ratio, or by mixing soy sauce 2:1 with some of the liquid from a tin of canned oysters. Neither will give you just the right taste and consistency, however. Vegetarian oyster sauces, often made with oyster mushrooms, and sometimes labeled "Vegetarian Stir-Fry Sauce," are available in many Asian stores.

## PALM SUGAR

The key source of sweetness in Thai cooking is traditionally palm sugar. Made from the concentrated sap of several different types of palm tree, palm sugar ranges in color from golden to dark brown and has a delicately caramelized flavor. It is available as either a thick, sticky paste (nam tan peep, น้ำตาลปีบ) or in harder, hockey puck–sized disks or spirals (nam tan pehrk, น้ำตาลปึก). The harder disks are more common outside of Thailand. Look for brands that are darker in color and appear moister and softer, as they are easier to use and have more flavor. To use the disk forms, soften them for a few minutes in the microwave on low power to make them easier to scoop and measure. For smaller amounts such as teaspoons and tablespoons, you can simply grate off as much as you need;

an advantage of grated palm sugar is that (unlike brown sugar or granulated sugar) it melts very quickly and easily when used in sauces and cooking. I've found that a small plastic container with a grating lid, intended for cheese, works very well for palm sugar, as any extra grated sugar can be stored for later use. Do not confuse palm sugar with coconut sugar (sometimes labeled "coconut palm sugar"), made from the flowers of coconut palm trees, which has a different taste and texture.

STORAGE: Lasts indefinitely in a cool, dry place.

SUBSTITUTES: You can use light or brown sugar, or sometimes plain granulated sugar, as a substitute. Each recipe will specify which substitutes are a good choice.

### PEPPER (PRIK THAI, พริกไทย)

Prior to the introduction of chile peppers from South America in the sixteenth century, white and black peppercorns were the primary source of spiciness in Thai cuisine. Thais primarily use white pepper (prik thai khao, พริกไทยขาว), which has a somewhat earthy, smoky flavor, and gives a true "Thai taste" to many dishes. As with all dried spices, it's preferable to buy them whole and grind them when ground pepper is called for, for maximum freshness and flavor.

STORAGE: Whole, dried spices will keep for several years in a cool, dark place.

SUBSTITUTES: Though it has a very different flavor, white pepper can be replaced by black pepper (prik thai dum, พริกไทยดำ) in any recipe in this book if you can't find white.

### ROASTED CHILI PASTE / CHILI JAM (NAM PRIK PAO, น้ำพริกเผา)

This rich, deep-red, oily paste, made from dried red chiles, is a key ingredient in Tom Yum Soup (page 93) as well as many stir-fries and sauces. Sometimes it is labeled as "Chili Paste in Soybean Oil." Some brands offer it in "mild," "medium," or "hot" spice levels.

STORAGE: Once opened, store in the refrigerator, where it will keep for several months.

SUBSTITUTES: To make your own, see the recipe on page 240.

## SOY SAUCE (SEE EW, ซีอิ๊ว)

Though it's used far less often than fish sauce in Thai cooking, soy sauce is essential for some Chinese-influenced specialties such as Kai Pa-Lo (Five Spice-Braised Chicken and Eggs, page 197) and many stir-fried dishes. There are three kinds of Thai soy sauce: "thin" or "light," "dark" or "black," and "dark sweet" or "black sweet" (see ew waan, ซีอิ๊วหวาน / see ew dum waan, ซีอิ๊วดำหวาน), a very thick, syrupy kind that tastes like soy sauce mixed with molasses.

Be careful not to confuse dark sweet soy sauce with "dark" or "black" soy sauce (see ew dum, ซีอิ๊วดำ), which is less sweet and used far less often than the other two types. Compare the Thai writing to the label to make sure. Thai soy sauces have a quite different taste and consistency than Japanese, Korean, Indonesian, and Chinese soy sauces, so look for Thai brands such as Healthy Boy. Any time a recipe in this book calls for "soy sauce," Thai "thin soy sauce" or "light soy sauce" is implied. Note that here "light" does not mean that it's a low-calorie version, simply that it is lighter in color.

STORAGE: Lasts indefinitely stored in a cool, dry place; refrigeration is not necessary.

SUBSTITUTES: If you can't find Thai light soy sauce, you can use Chinese soy sauce. If you can't find Thai dark sweet soy sauce, you can approximate it by mixing 1 tablespoon Thai light soy sauce or Chinese soy sauce with 1 tablespoon palm sugar or brown sugar and 1 teaspoon dark molasses; use the resulting mixture as a 1:1 replacement for dark sweet soy sauce in any recipe.

## VINEGAR (NAM SOM, น้ำส้ม)

Vinegar is a common ingredient for its bright sourness. Thais usually use basic distilled white vinegar, which is easy to find and inexpensive. It also doesn't alter the color of sauces. If you use rice vinegar, be sure to use an unseasoned one, with no sugar added.

STORAGE: Keeps indefinitely in a cool, dark cupboard.

SUBSTITUTES: Unseasoned rice vinegar or white wine vinegar.

## THE "THREE PALS" OF THAI COOKING

Much like *soffritto* (Italian) or *mirepoix* (French), that "holy trinity" mixture of finely chopped carrot, celery, and onion that is the base for countless sauces, soups, and other dishes in Italian and French cuisine, Thai cooking has its own starter base, *saam glehr* (three pals), consisting of white peppercorns, cilantro root, and garlic. The paste, mashed together in a granite mortar and pestle, is the secret ingredient that gives so many dishes their distinctly, unmistakably "Thai" flavor. Since cilantro root can be difficult to find, as most non-Thai grocers cut them off before sale, the bottom few inches of cilantro stems are the closest substitute.

## FRESH HERBS AND AROMATICS

### BASIL

Several different varieties of fresh basil are used in Thai cooking, both as an ingredient and a garnish. We will use only two in this book:

**THAI BASIL / SWEET BASIL** (horapa, โหระพา) With smaller, more pointed leaves than Italian sweet basil, this basil has purple stems and flowers and a more savory taste, with hints of anise and licorice.

**HOLY BASIL / HOT BASIL** (ga phrao, กะเพรา) This basil has hairy stems and small, pointed, light green leaves with serrated edges, sometimes with a reddish tint. It's pungent and aromatic and has a spicy, peppery taste with hints of mint and clove. It's used in the popular dishes Pad Ga Phrao Gai (Stir-Fried Chicken with Basil, page 195), where it is stir-fried with meats, seafood, or vegetables, and in Pad Kee Mao (Spicy Drunken Noodles, page 81).

**STORAGE:** Refrigerate, wrapped in damp paper towels and then in plastic or upright in a glass of water, for up to one week.

**SUBSTITUTES:** You can substitute Italian sweet basil for both varieties of Thai basil in a pinch. Both Thai sweet and holy basil, however, are available in Asian markets in glass jars in premixed chili sauces for stir-fries, for a more authentic flavor, if you can't find them fresh.

## CHILES (PRIK, พริก)

There are many different types of chile pepper in Thailand, but for this book, in addition to dried chiles, we'll use just two of the most common:

BIRD'S-EYE CHILES / BIRD CHILES / THAI CHILES (prik khi nu, พริกขี้หนู) These tiny, fiery peppers are usually about an inch long, or the size of a fingertip (though some US growers produce 2- to 3-inch-long bird chiles). Their Thai name translates to "mouse-dropping chile." They range in color from emerald green to fire-engine red, with the younger green peppers being the spiciest, though the mature red ones are only somewhat milder. They are often sold as "Thai chiles." Though not quite as spicy as habaneros, they are far spicier than jalapeños. They're used in many curries, salads, sauces, and condiments, often in a mixture of both red and green.

LONG CHILES (prik chi fa, พริกชี้ฟ้า) Milder than bird chiles, these are about the size of a finger, or 3 to 4 inches in length. Often used in stir-fries, they can be red, green, or orange-yellow.

DRIED CHILES (prik haeng, พริกแห้ง) Several different kinds are used, in a range of sizes. In general, the larger the chile, the milder the spice level.

STORAGE: Wrapped in a paper bag, fresh chiles will last about a week in the crisper drawer of a refrigerator. They do not freeze well, quickly losing their texture and pungent spice.

SUBSTITUTES: For bird chiles, you can substitute fresh chile de árbol, Fresno, or cayenne peppers. If those aren't available either, serrano peppers (preferable) or jalapeños can be used. For long chiles, serrano peppers are a good equivalent, both in heat level and size. Any dried chile peppers can be used in these recipes, with the general rule of thumb that the smaller they are, the spicier.

## CILANTRO (PAK CHI, ผักชี), CILANTRO ROOTS, AND CORIANDER SEEDS

Fresh cilantro (also known as coriander) is another of the pillars of Thai cuisine. But the true "secret ingredient" that gives authentic Thai flavor to many dishes is the root of the plant, rather than the leaves. Unfortunately, outside of Thailand, the root is typically removed before sale since it is not an ingredient used in any other cuisine. When you do find cilantro with the roots still attached, it's a good idea to buy as much of it as you can, since you can freeze the roots (after cleaning and chopping them) and use them as-is, without defrosting. Some online stores sell only the roots. Coriander seed is used in many curry pastes and other dishes and has a warm, nutty, citrusy flavor.

STORAGE: Refrigerate fresh cilantro, wrapped in damp paper towels and then in plastic or placed upright in a glass of water, for up to one week. Cilantro roots will keep in the freezer for up to six months. Whole coriander seeds will keep for several years in a cool, dark place.

SUBSTITUTES: If you can't find the roots, use the bottom inch or so of the stems (without any leaves). There is no substitute for cilantro leaves or coriander seeds.

## GALANGAL (KHA, ข่า)

Galangal is a rhizome, like ginger, and the two are related and similar in appearance, though galangal is smaller, with thinner skin and a reddish-pinkish hue. Their flavors are completely different, however, and ginger cannot be used as a substitute. Galangal has a subtle, delicate flavor, fresh and somewhat reminiscent of a pine forest. It's a key ingredient in many curry pastes as well as the popular Tom Kha Gai (Coconut-Galangal Soup with Chicken, page 95).

STORAGE: Wrapped in paper towels and refrigerated in a plastic bag in the crisper, galangal lasts for several weeks. Thinly sliced (⅛ inch thick) and wrapped in plastic, it can be frozen for several months, though texture and taste will suffer a bit.

SUBSTITUTES: There is no substitute. Dried or powdered galangal can't match the flavor of fresh or frozen, but if that is all that is available, it is better than nothing. Even though they are similar in appearance, ginger or *grachai* (fingerroot) are very different in flavor and can't be used as substitutes. If you can't find galangal in any form, it's better to omit it than use ginger instead.

## GARLIC (GRATIEM, กระเทียม)

A great deal of garlic is used in Thai cooking, and it is almost always minced very finely. Avoid the temptation to buy jars of chopped garlic or garlic paste, as it loses its flavor and pungency quickly after chopping.

## KAFFIR LIME / KAFFIR LIME LEAVES (MAKRUT / BAI MAKRUT, มะกรูด/ใบมะกรูด)

The unique "double" leaves of kaffir limes resemble two shiny, dark-green leaves fused to each other at one end, and they are partially responsible for the distinctive flavor of Tom Yum Soup (page 93), among other dishes.

**STORAGE:** Store fresh fruits and leaves in the refrigerator and use within a few days. The fruit, zest, and leaves can be wrapped in plastic and frozen for several months.

**SUBSTITUTES:** There is no substitute. Avoid dried kaffir lime leaves, as they have very little flavor. Frozen leaves, however, are a good option when you can't find fresh ones.

## LEMONGRASS (TAKHRAI, ตะไคร้)

These woody stalks, with their fresh citronella fragrance, are a key ingredient in many Thai curry pastes, soups, stir-fries, and salads.

Only the tender interior of the bottom three inches is used (peel away and discard the tougher outer layers). You can infuse boiling water with the remaining parts to make lemongrass tea.

**STORAGE:** Store in the refrigerator crisper, wrapped well in plastic to keep it from drying out, for up to one week. If you are planning to use it for curry paste or soups, lemongrass freezes well and will keep for several months in the freezer, wrapped in plastic wrap and stored in a resealable freezer bag; you can use it directly from the freezer, without defrosting. Frozen lemongrass is not as good for salads, as the texture gets a bit mushy when thawed.

**SUBSTITUTES:** Dried or powdered lemongrass is not as flavorful or complex as fresh; it will do in a pinch for curries and soups, but can't be used in stir-fries or salads. Lemongrass paste is also available in tubes or jars in some stores. Again, it's not as good as fresh and is not ideal for soups or salads, but it can be a timesaver for curry pastes or stir-fries. Frozen sliced or ground lemongrass can be found in some supermarkets and Asian markets and is a great option for curry pastes.

## LIMES (MANOW, มะนาว)

A key source of the "sour" flavor in Thai cooking. Lemons are not used in Thai cuisine, and do not give the same flavor, but can be used if limes are unavailable or prohibitively expensive. Don't use bottled lime juice, which lacks the same fresh flavor and complexity.

**STORAGE:** Store fresh fruits and leaves in the refrigerator and use within a few days. The fruit, zest, and leaves can be wrapped in plastic and frozen for several months.

**SUBSTITUTES:** There is no substitute.

## SHALLOTS (HOM DAENG, หอมแดง)

Shallots are used far more often than onions in Thai cuisine, in curry pastes, in salads, and, when fried crisp, as a garnish. They are milder than onions, with a more complex flavor, so they are more agreeable when used raw.

**STORAGE:** Store in a cool, dark place for several weeks, or up to one month.

**SUBSTITUTES:** Shallots are available most everywhere these days, but if you can't find them, you can use red onions instead. Fried shallots, such as Hánh Phi and Nang Fah brands, can be found in Asian markets.

## TAMARIND (MAKHAM, มะขาม)

This tangy, sweet-and-sour fruit is used in many sauces and is a key ingredient in authentic Pad Thai. The concentrated reddish-brown pulp is sold in solid blocks in clear plastic packets in most Asian markets (look for brands imported from Thailand that contain only 100% tamarind, with no additives). It might be labeled "wet tamarind," "tamarind juice," "concentrated tamarind juice," or "seedless tamarind." Even when labeled "seedless," however, it almost always still contains some seeds, hull, and bits of stringy membrane and so will need to be reconstituted and strained before use (see page 26). It's also available as tamarind paste, in glass jars with the seeds already removed, which doesn't taste as fresh but is much easier and faster to use. Be sure not to buy dried or candied whole tamarind fruit or pastes that have sugar or salt added. The only ingredient should be tamarind.

**STORAGE:** Store opened tamarind paste or pulp in the refrigerator for up to one month.

**SUBSTITUTES:** If you can't find tamarind, its tangy character can be loosely approximated by a mixture of equal parts fresh lime juice and water.

# Other Ingredients of the Thai Pantry

The following ingredients, while nice to have on hand, will be essential for only one or two dishes, or, if they are more difficult to find outside of Thai communities, can easily be substituted by more common ingredients. If you plan to stick to using store-bought curry pastes, you might never need some of these since they are necessary for homemade curry pastes.

BEAN SPROUTS (tua ngoc, ถั่วงอก) The young, crisp-tender sprout of the mung bean plant, these are an essential topping for Pad Thai (page 72) and other noodle dishes. Soak them in cold water for 10 minutes before using, and then drain well for extra crispness. They will keep, refrigerated, for up to one week in a plastic bag.

CHINESE BROCCOLI (pak kha na, ผักคะน้า) Like the Italian broccoli most familiar in the United States, Chinese broccoli, or *gai lan*, is a member of the mustard family. Its taste and texture, however, are closer to that of broccoli rabe, which makes a good substitute. If you can't find broccoli rabe either, then mustard greens, collard greens, broccolini, or broccoli can be used, in order of preference.

DRIED SHRIMP (goong haeng, กุ้งแห้ง) These tiny (about ½ inch long) shrimp are salted and dried and are used in many curry pastes and in popular Thai dishes such as Pad Thai (page 72) and Som Tum (Green Papaya Salad, page 99). They are sold in bags in Asian markets and are often found in the refrigerated or frozen section. Choose frozen or refrigerated if you have a choice, since they will be fresher as well as more tender and flavorful. Look for ones with no added preservatives and that look plump and pink, rather than shriveled and white. They can be refrigerated for several weeks or frozen for several months. You can use frozen dried shrimp directly in recipes, without defrosting.

EGGPLANT There are many kinds of eggplant in Thailand, in various shapes and sizes. They are often used as ingredients in curries or eaten raw with dips.

> PEA EGGPLANT (makhuea puang, มะเขือพวง) As their name indicates, these tiny round eggplants resemble green peas, which make a fine substitute for them as a curry ingredient, at least in terms of appearance—the taste is quite different.

THAI EGGPLANT (makhuea proh, มะเขือเปราะ) These round, green-and-white eggplants are about the size of a golf ball. To substitute, use either long Asian eggplants or Italian or globe eggplants, cut into 1- to 2-inch chunks.

FERMENTED SOYBEAN / YELLOW BEAN SAUCE (tow jiew, เต้าเจี้ยว) This sauce is a key ingredient in the gravy for Rad Na noodles (Stir-Fried Rice Noodles with Gravy, page 78) and in some other stir-fried dishes. Some brands are thicker than others, but all should feature whole soybean halves in a brownish or yellowish liquid. If you can't find a Thai brand, Chinese tai hua, salted or preserved soybeans, can be used instead. Once opened, it keeps indefinitely in the refrigerator.

FINGERROOT (grachai, กระชาย) Made up of a cluster of long, thin, knobby "fingers," this pale-yellow rhizome goes by many other names, including wild ginger and Chinese keys. It has a bright, somewhat medicinal flavor. It's used in some curry pastes and in many seafood dishes. You can find it fresh or frozen in Asian markets or sometimes jarred in brine, either whole or in thin slices. It can't be substituted by either galangal or ginger, so if you can't find it, you can simply omit it.

FIVE-SPICE POWDER (pong pa-lo, ผงพะโล้) A mix of spices (mixes vary, but generally the Thai versions contain coriander, star anise, allspice, cinnamon, and bay leaves) used in Chinese-influenced dishes such as Kai Pa-Lo (Five Spice–Braised Chicken and Eggs, page 197).

GINGER (khing, ขิง) This piquant, knobby rhizome is not used that often in Thai cuisine. It appears chiefly in dishes of Chinese origin, such as Stir-Fried Ginger Chicken (page 191). Young ginger, sold in Asian grocery stores, is tender and thin-skinned and doesn't require peeling before use. It's interchangeable with regular ginger root in recipes. Unpeeled ginger root can be refrigerated for up to three weeks or frozen for up to six months. Ginger paste is available in tubes or jars in some places. It's not as good as fresh, but it can be a timesaver and a good thing to keep on hand for use in a pinch. Dried, powdered ginger, however, cannot approximate the taste or texture of fresh.

GREEN PAPAYA (malakoh dip, มะละกอดิบ) Crisp, unripe green papaya is the key ingredient in the popular, spicy Som Tum salad (page 99) from Northeastern Thailand. It should be stored at room temperature but used soon (within a day or two), as it will ripen and soften quickly. If you can't find green papaya, you can use carrots, jicama, green (unripe) mango, green apples, or any combination thereof.

MINT (bai saranaah, ใบสะระแหน่) Fresh mint leaves mostly appear in salads from the Isaan region, such as Lahb (page 110). Mint can be stored upright in the fridge in a jar of water, just like cilantro and basil. Do not use dried mint as a substitute for fresh in salads.

PEANUTS / PEANUT BUTTER (tua lisong, ถั่วลิสง) Crushed peanuts are often used as a garnish for dipping sauce, in Pad Thai (page 72), and in other dishes. Use roasted, unsalted peanuts for Thai cooking. Traditionally, ground peanuts are used in some curry pastes and sauces, but you can use peanut butter instead for convenience. Choose natural, unsweetened peanut butters, the kind with oil floating on top, and avoid those with added sugar or emulsifiers.

RICE PAPER WRAPPERS (bánh tráng in Vietnamese) These are used for making Fresh Spring Rolls (page 37). Look for large, round (about 8 to 9 inches in diameter), translucent white sheets. They are dried, not refrigerated, and must be reconstituted briefly in warm water before use.

ROASTED RICE POWDER (khao kua, ข้าวคั่ว) Also known as "toasted rice powder," this is a truly essential ingredient for Lahb (page 110), the traditional Isaan salad made with fresh herbs and minced meat, as well as many other dishes from Northeastern Thailand. It's available in Asian markets, but you can also make your own by toasting uncooked sticky rice (preferable) or jasmine rice over low heat in a dry skillet, shaking the skillet constantly until evenly golden brown (but not burned), 10 to 15 minutes. Then let it cool completely and grind it to a fine powder either in a mortar and pestle with a circular motion or using a spice grinder. The texture should resemble coarse cornmeal. It will keep in an airtight jar in a cool, dark, dry place for up to one month.

SALTED RADISH (hua chai bpo, หัวไชโป๊ว) Finely chopped radish, preserved in salt, is a traditional ingredient in classic Pad Thai (page 72) and can be served on top of plain rice soup or Rice Porridge (page 62). It adds a chewy texture and savory, slightly sweet taste. It's sold in strips or chopped in vacuum-sealed clear plastic bags in Asian markets, usually unrefrigerated. It's sometimes labeled as "preserved radish," "pickled turnip," or any combination of these names. It keeps indefinitely in an airtight container and does not need to be refrigerated.

SEASONING SAUCE (sauce pu khao thong, ซอสภูเขาทอง) A distinctively Thai sauce, its taste falls somewhere between soy sauce and fish sauce, and yet is not the same as either. It's a "secret ingredient" for giving truly authentic Thai taste to any number of dishes but most often is used as a table sauce, much the way soy sauce is used in Chinese dining. Golden Mountain and Maggi brands are interchangeable, though Golden Mountain is more quintessentially Thai. It keeps indefinitely at room temperature.

**SHRIMP PASTE** (gapi, กะปิ) Many Thai foods are notorious for their somewhat overpowering smell, but besides durian fruit, gapi is possibly the most off-putting. But don't let that prevent you from using it because, used in small quantities, this pungent, smooth tan or grayish paste made from fermented, ground shrimp is an essential ingredient in many Thai curry pastes and sauces. In other words, if you're a fan of Thai food, you've probably already unknowingly consumed gapi on many occasions. Try to look past its potent funk, because it is also a powerful ally in the kitchen. Once opened, a jar will last (tightly sealed!) in the refrigerator for several months. Although it is related to fermented shrimp pastes used in other Southeast Asian cuisines, such as belachan (Malaysia) and bagoong (Philippines), the tastes and textures are different. Do not confuse it with "shrimp paste in soybean oil," which looks red and liquidy in the jar; gapi is dry, grayish-purple, and pasty. Anchovy paste would be a very approximate substitution. Some use Vegemite or Marmite as a vegan substitute.

**SRIRACHA SAUCE** (sauce Sriracha, ซอสศรีราชา) Previously unknown outside of Thai communities, this tangy, bright-orange hot sauce made with fresh long chiles has in recent years rocketed to cult-like status. However, the brand most Americans are familiar with, Huy Fong, known as "rooster sauce" and produced in California by a Vietnamese owner, contains preservatives and has a quite different taste and texture than the original Thai sauce, which is thinner, sweeter, and more balanced in flavor. For Thai cooking, look for Thai brands (preferably from the coastal town of Sri Racha, Thailand, where the sauce originates) that contain only chiles, sugar, garlic, vinegar, and salt, with no preservatives or other additives. Shark brand is a good one to look out for. Sriracha is a very versatile sauce but it pairs particularly well with seafood, egg, or meat dishes. Opened bottles will keep in the refrigerator for many months.

**SWEET CHILI SAUCE / CHICKEN SAUCE** (nam jim gai, น้ำจิ้มไก่) A thick, sweet-spicy dipping sauce traditionally served with Thai-style grilled chicken, it can also be used as a dipping sauce for spring rolls, fried tofu, and fried wontons. A good store-bought brand is Mae Ploy. To make your own, see the recipe on page 239.

**TURMERIC** (kameen, ขมิ้น) Fresh turmeric, a small, bright-orange rhizome, is used in many curry pastes and soups, particularly those originating from southern Thailand. Wrap fresh turmeric in a dry paper towel and then store in a resealable plastic bag in the refrigerator for up to two months. If you can't find fresh turmeric, use ½ teaspoon dried, powdered turmeric for each 1-inch fresh piece or 1 teaspoon minced fresh turmeric. Fresh turmeric has a sweeter, less medicinal flavor.

**WONTON WRAPPERS / SPRING ROLL WRAPPERS** (paen hoh geaw, แผ่นห่อเกี๊ยว)  These can be found in almost any Asian grocery store, and in well-stocked supermarkets, in the refrigerated or frozen section. If using frozen, defrost overnight in the refrigerator. The wrappers come in different sizes; for wontons, use 4-inch square wrappers; for fried spring rolls, use 6-inch square (or round, which works just as well) wrappers. "Egg roll" wrappers, which contain egg, will puff up when fried, while spring roll wrappers remain smooth after frying. You can use either. When rolling, keep the unused stack covered with a damp, clean kitchen towel to prevent them from drying out.

**YOUNG GREEN PEPPERCORNS** (prik thai ohn, พริกไทยอ่อน)  Sold in the refrigerated produce section of Asian markets, fresh young green peppercorns resemble tiny bunches of green grapes and are an ingredient in Jungle Curry (page 138) and other dishes. The branches are used whole in cooking, though only the peppercorns are edible; they add pleasant crunch and a fragrant spiciness. You can also use the jarred kind, packed in brine; simply drain them and use the same way in any recipe.

## "THAI SPICY"

In Thailand, people don't usually specify the spice level for a dish when ordering. The dishes are just made as they usually are—some are inherently quite fiery; others are traditionally very mild. But there is always a condiment caddy on the table—usually containing granulated sugar, chopped chiles in vinegar, lime juice, or fish sauce and ground chili powder—to allow diners to adjust the spiciness and other flavors to their own liking. In this book, the spice levels indicate how hot a recipe is when prepared as written. Of course, you can always adjust the heat levels by adding more or less curry paste or chiles; removing (or leaving in) the chile seeds, which are the hottest part of the pepper; or using any of the many dipping sauces and condiments in chapter 11 to adjust the spice level on individual portions.

# Basic Kitchen Tools

Aside from absolute kitchen essentials like a good chef's knife and a paring knife, just a few basic tools can help guarantee easier prep and better results for your Thai cooking. That said, none of these are essential—you really don't need a lot of fancy equipment for most everyday Thai cooking.

MORTAR AND PESTLE A fully equipped traditional Thai kitchen would have a granite mortar and pestle for all-purpose use and a large, clay mortar with a long wooden pestle for making Som Tum (Green Papaya Salad, page 99). If I were to choose only one tool for Thai cooking, it would be a smooth granite mortar and pestle. Many Thai dishes are based on aromatic pastes, and the best tool for the job is a mortar. It is invaluable for making curry pastes, grinding whole spices, crushing nuts, and more, and a blender or food processor doesn't give the same texture and taste. In addition, with the small amounts of ingredients you will usually be working with, it can be difficult to create pastes in a blender or food processor.

Thai granite mortar-and-pestle sets are sold in many Asian markets as well as online (see Resources, page 250) and are usually quite inexpensive. Look for one with a bowl at least 6 inches in diameter and relatively deep. If you choose to use a blender or food processor instead, you might need to add small amounts of water to facilitate grinding, or double or triple the recipe so that you're working with larger volumes. For small amounts of dry ingredients, an electric spice grinder or coffee grinder can be used. A blender or handheld immersion blender (some come with a small container attachment for grinding small amounts of ingredients) is preferable to a food processor for making curry pastes, as they deal better with the smaller volumes of ingredients.

WOK Besides a granite mortar and pestle, a well-seasoned carbon-steel wok could be your greatest ally for Thai cooking. It's difficult to make certain stir-fried dishes, particularly noodle dishes, well without a seasoned (see page 24) wok, though you can make do with a large (14-inch) sauté pan or skillet instead. A wok cooks quickly, sears ingredients while cooking, and gives the best flavor. It's also great for deep-frying, since it requires far less oil than a pot. They're usually quite inexpensive in Asian markets ($10 to $20).

Look for one about 14 inches in diameter, with a wooden handle, a helper handle across from the main handle, and a flat bottom. It's best to use woks or skillets without a nonstick coating for stir-frying, as the high heats required for stir-frying can release toxic chemicals from some nonstick coatings. Woks work better with gas stoves than electric, though a flat-bottomed wok can be used on an electric stovetop as well. All stir-fry recipes in this book were developed using a carbon-steel wok on a gas stove, so if you are using a skillet or an electric or induction stove, you might need to increase cooking times in these recipes.

# Optional Tools

These tools are nice to have and can make preparing Thai meals easier, but they aren't a necessity.

**CHARCOAL OR HIBACHI GRILL**  For the grilled recipes in this book, an outdoor charcoal grill is ideal, but you can also use a gas grill or a stovetop grill pan. Some can be roasted in an oven instead.

**CHOPSTICKS OR BAMBOO TONGS**  When browning or frying many small, individual pieces, I find a long pair of wooden or bamboo chopsticks quite useful for turning them so that they brown evenly on all sides. Tongs, while a bit clumsier, can serve the same purpose.

**JULIENNE SLICER**  This handheld tool resembles a vegetable peeler, but with a corrugated blade that is perfect for creating the long, thin strands of green papaya and carrots needed for Som Tum (page 99) and other salads. A popular, inexpensive Thai brand called Kiwi Pro Slice is easy to find online and in many Asian markets. Alternatively, you can use a handheld grater or box grater or a food processor with a grater attachment.

**KITCHEN SCALE** This is not as essential for Thai cooking as it is for baking, but as kitchen scales are inexpensive, small, and useful for any type of cooking, it certainly doesn't hurt to have one.

**MANDOLINE SLICER** These are really handy for saving a lot of time and hassle when you need to prepare a large amount of very thinly sliced vegetables or aromatics, such as when making curry paste or a salad.

**RICE COOKER** I don't consider an electric rice cooker a must; in fact, I haven't owned one for years, though I eat rice very often. But if you have the space for one, they can certainly save some stress and stovetop space. Their advantages include that they prevent a layer of burned or overcooked rice on the bottom of the pot, they can keep the rice warm while you prepare other dishes, and some modern, advanced versions have porridge or congee settings.

**SPIDER SKIMMER / STRAINER** This tool is quite useful to have for deep frying. Inexpensive ones, with bamboo handles, are usually available at Asian markets.

**STEAMER** Either a stacking metal stovetop steamer, a bamboo steamer, or a jerry-rigged steamer (a fine-mesh strainer inserted in a covered pot above simmering water) will be sufficient for most Thai cooking.

**STICKY RICE STEAMER BASKET AND POT** In Thailand, sticky rice is traditionally steamed in a special cone-shaped woven bamboo basket set into an accompanying urn-shaped metal pot. This setup is generally inexpensive, with the bamboo imparting an authentic fragrance to the steamed rice. However, it also takes up a lot of space, so if you have a small kitchen and limited storage space, it is certainly a piece of single-use equipment you can do without. Alternative methods for steaming sticky rice are provided in this book.

**THAI TEA FILTER** Thai tea is traditionally brewed by straining through a long, tapered muslin "sock" attached to a stainless-steel loop with a handle. These are inexpensive and sold in Asian markets or online. You can skip it, however, and filter the tea through finely woven cheesecloth or a coffee filter instead.

# Getting Technical: Thai Cooking Techniques and Tips

In general, Thai cooking techniques are not that different from those used for most other Asian cuisines–there's lots of stir-frying, as well as simmering, steaming, braising, grilling, and some deep-frying. Traditional Thai kitchens don't have ovens, so there's not a lot of baking or oven-roasting (Who would want to use an oven in Thai heat and humidity?). Any key differences unique to Thai cooking are outlined below.

1. **GETTING READY** The French culinary term *mise en place*, meaning "put in place," refers to getting all of the ingredients required for a dish prepped and measured before you start cooking. It's a very important step for any type of cuisine, because once you have everything ready, you'll find that everything else just falls into place and even seemingly complicated recipes become simple. It's particularly important, however, for Thai cooking, especially stir-frying, because in stir-frying everything happens very quickly once you start cooking, and if everything isn't ready to go before you start, it's easy to wind up with burned food or other kitchen disasters. When stir-frying, I arrange all of the prepped and measured ingredients in the order in which they'll go into the wok, so that I don't even have to refer to the recipe when cooking. Asian markets often sell inexpensive small saucers and bowls that are perfect for holding prepped ingredients.

2. **PREPPING AND SAUTÉING GARLIC** If you are new to Asian cooking, there are some key differences to understand, before you begin, between the way garlic is prepared and cooked in European and other Western cuisines and the way it is used in Southeast Asian cooking. Rather than being used in whole cloves or large slices, as is often done, for example, in Italian cooking, garlic is almost always either very finely minced or crushed and used as a paste in Thai cuisine. When used in stir-fries, this finely minced garlic is added once the cooking oil is hot and shimmering and then sautéed until a golden brown. It should seem almost burned. Be careful, though–there is a fine line between well browned and burned with garlic, as burned garlic has a bitter, acrid taste. Until you get the hang of it, you might need to discard some burned garlic and start over, but it is important for an authentic Thai taste to cook the garlic till golden brown.

3. **POUNDING AND GRINDING** When pulverizing moist ingredients in a mortar and pestle or in a blender, a pinch of salt can help break them down. If you've never used a mortar and pestle, it can take a little getting used to the technique. Pound at a 45-degree angle until larger ingredients are broken down, and then switch to a circular grinding motion, using the pestle to press ingredients against the walls of the mortar. Place a quilted pot holder or folded kitchen towel underneath your mortar to muffle the noise and protect your counter; for extra protection, place the towel or pot holder on top of a wooden cutting board.

4. **CRACKING COCONUT MILK** Probably the single most important technique to master for authentic Thai curries is getting the coconut milk to "crack" (or have the oil separate from the milk) before adding the rest of the curry ingredients. Thai curries traditionally have a thin layer of oil, or at least droplets of oil, floating on top, though in some US restaurants curry might not be made that way, either to cater to more Western concepts of food presentation or because only homogenized coconut milk (which has had emulsifiers added so that the fats will not separate out of the milk) is available for the cooks to use. It is preferable not only for aesthetics, but also for the best mouthfeel, to temper the spiciness, and to prevent any leftover curry from drying out when stored. Here are some tips for success:

- Look for coconut milks that do not have added emulsifiers or stabilizers, such as guar gum, which prevent separation.

- Do not shake the can (or box) of coconut milk before using. The cream naturally rises to the top in unemulsified milk, and that is what you will need to start your curry. Storing the can in the refrigerator for an hour before use can help the cream separate out, if it hasn't already.

- After opening the can, use a spoon to skim the solid layer of cream off the top. Simmer it over medium heat together with the curry paste, without stirring, until tiny pockets of oil start to separate out from the cream. You will see these little pools of oil appear where the simmering bubbles are and take on the color of whatever curry paste you're using. At the same time, the mixture will grow thicker and drier.

- Be patient. It might take up to about 10 minutes for the cream to crack.

- Don't despair if you've followed these instructions carefully and the cream still will not crack. Sometimes, even when using the right kind of milk and the right technique, the milk simply won't crack. It's not a disaster. See the next tip.

- If all else fails and your coconut cream and curry paste mixture simply will not crack, you can either simply skip to the next step, or you can "cheat" a little by adding a bit (about 1 tablespoon) of unrefined coconut oil (preferable) or vegetable oil, simmering for 1 minute longer, and then continuing with the recipe.

**5. CUTTING CUCUMBERS** There is a whole tradition of fruit and vegetable carving in Thailand, with very elaborate, artistic patterns. That is not something we'll cover in this book, but a very simple technique for making cucumber "flowers" as garnishes is very low effort but makes a big impression: Cut four or five long, V-shaped pieces (about ⅛ inch wide) lengthwise out of the peel of a cucumber, spaced evenly around the outside. Then when you cut it crosswise into ¼-inch thick slices, each will resemble a small flower.

**6. SEASONING, USING, AND MAINTAINING A CARBON-STEEL WOK** A new carbon-steel wok must be seasoned before use, but like a cast iron skillet, if you season it correctly and take good care of it, it will eventually develop a naturally nonstick black coating that improves the flavor of any dish you cook in it. Here's how to season it the first time:

- Scrub the new pan well, inside and out, with steel wool, dish soap, and warm water to remove the oil coating it is sold with. Rinse and dry it well, and then place it on a burner over low heat for 1 to 2 minutes to finish drying completely.

- Turn the burner to high heat, and heat the wok well. When a few drops of water flicked onto the surface sizzle and evaporate immediately, it is ready.

- Remove the wok from the heat and add about 2 tablespoons of a neutral, high-smoke-point oil such as peanut oil, refined coconut oil, or grapeseed oil (don't use canola oil, which can develop a fishy flavor at high temperatures). Swirl the pan to coat the surface evenly with the oil.

- Add a handful of fresh, unpeeled ginger slices (¼ inch thick) and a handful of roughly chopped scallions.

- Return to the stove, turn the heat to medium, and stir-fry for 5 to 10 minutes, using a wooden spoon or spatula to mash the scallions and ginger and rub them over the entire surface of the wok.

- A multicolored patina should form on the surface (it's okay if it's uneven; that's normal). Discard the aromatics, let the pan cool, rinse well with hot water, and dry completely over low heat.

- Stir-fry techniques: After heating cooking oil in your wok, swirl the oil around to coat the surface evenly before adding any ingredients. Thai dishes are usually stir-fried at a lower temperature than in Chinese cooking, but it is still important to stir continuously to prevent the ingredients from sticking or burning. Use a wooden spoon or spatula to prevent scratching or damaging the patina.

- To maintain your seasoned wok: Never use dish soap or abrasive scrubbers to wash it again, only hot water and a soft sponge or brush. If there is cooked-on food, you can soak it in hot water for 10 minutes before scrubbing. If the surface gets sticky, you can use salt mixed with vegetable oil to scrub the wok while it is still warm, using a paper towel. Be sure to dry the wok well on a low burner after each rinsing to avoid rusting. If you won't be using it for

## THAI SPELLING

I've often been asked why there are so many different spellings in English for the same Thai words. Which is correct? Basically, written Thai uses an alphabet with many more consonants (forty-four) than English has, as well as a complex vowel system and five tones. All that is extremely difficult to convey when transliterated into a Latin alphabet. Although official standards—such as the Royal Thai General System of Transcription (RTGS) and the standard from the International Organization for Standardization (ISO)—exist, they have some limitations, and they are not consistently applied, leading to a great deal of confusion. In this book, I have, to some degree, followed the standards, but I've also made my own decisions on how to represent names to best give English-speaking readers an idea, within the limitations, of how words are actually pronounced.

a while, you can also rub the wok's surface (inside and out) with a paper towel moistened with a little vegetable oil before storing it. Do not cook highly acidic foods (such as vinegar) in a new wok as they will strip your carefully built-up patina.

7. **WORKING WITH CHILES** The seeds are the hottest part of any chile pepper, since they contain the most capsaicin. So, for milder bite in any recipe calling for fresh chiles, remove the seeds before use. Be careful to wash your hands with soap and cold water immediately after handling cut chiles, and avoid touching your face or eyes. This seems like a common-sense rule, but I'd be embarrassed to admit the number of times I've absentmindedly rubbed my eyes after cutting chiles and then instantly regretted it. You can also wear disposable rubber gloves when handling them, if you have extremely sensitive skin or think you'll be likely to forget. If you get chile oil on your hands and it won't wash out with soap and water, I've found that rubbing alcohol (isopropyl alcohol) is far more effective.

8. **USING DRIED AND FRESH NOODLES** Dried rice or bean thread noodles will usually need to be soaked in hot or warm water for a few minutes before use. Depending on how they will be used in a recipe, you might need to then blanch them in boiling water and drain them well, or they might be used directly, for example, in spring rolls. Fresh noodles, on the other hand, can be used directly, without a presoak. If they are not ultra-fresh, however, you might need to soften them for a bit in a microwave, in 30-second increments, for about 1 to 2 minutes, until they can be easily separated into individual strands (use your hands for this). See page 74 for more information on using dried rice noodles.

9. **PREPARING TAMARIND PASTE FROM CONCENTRATED PULP** Sweet and tangy tamarind fruit is a key ingredient in many Thai recipes for its bright, sour taste. Though you can find jarred, ready-to-use tamarind paste in Asian markets, concentrated tamarind pulp, sold in solid blocks in clear plastic packaging, is the best choice for the freshest flavor. Even those that are labeled "without seed," however, usually contain bits of seed, hull, and stringy membrane and need to be softened in water and then strained before use in recipes. Here's how:

- Immerse the block of tamarind in a bowl of warm water (about 2 tablespoons warm water per ounce of solid seedless tamarind pulp).

- Let sit for about 15 minutes, and then mix well, using your fingers, to help the pulp dissolve.

- Strain through a fine-mesh strainer, using a rubber spatula or the bottom of a ladle to push all the pulp through the mesh, leaving behind the seeds and stringy bits. Squeeze the remaining bits tightly in your hand to extract all the pulp, and then discard.

- The resulting liquid can be used in any of the recipes in this book calling for "tamarind paste." A 5.3-ounce block of tamarind pulp treated this way will yield about ½ cup homemade tamarind paste. It will keep, in a sealed glass jar in the refrigerator, for up to one week or in the freezer for up to six months.

# CHAPTER TWO

# Snacks and Starters

Thai people love to snack outside meals, at pretty much any hour of the day or night, and since there are street stalls all over Thailand selling delicious fried, steamed, or grilled treats, quick nibbles are never more than a few steps away. But for those living in places with no sidewalk hawkers, many of these snacks are incredibly quick and simple, requiring only a few ingredients and less than 15 minutes of your time–prep and cook time included! They all make great appetizers before a meal, finger foods for a party, or anytime snacks. Some can even become a quick, light meal when accompanied by some Jasmine Rice (page 53) or Sticky Rice (page 55).

# Spring Rolls Versus Egg Rolls Versus Wontons

What's the difference between wonton wrappers, spring roll wrappers, and egg roll wrappers? First off, they have different sizes and shapes. Wonton wrappers are generally about 4 inches square, while spring roll wrappers can range in size from 5 inches up to around 10 inches. Spring roll wrappers can be square or round, while wonton wrappers are always square. Egg roll wrappers, as you might guess from the name, contain egg and are generally larger than spring roll wrappers. Look for wonton wrappers with a rich yellowish-brown color that are made with eggs, but without food coloring. Spring roll wrappers remain smooth when fried, while egg roll wrappers puff up. You can use them interchangeably, but just be aware of that main difference. All three are sold in the refrigerated or frozen section of Asian markets, or sometimes in mainstream supermarkets, near the tofu section (but wrappers will usually be fresher, higher-quality, and cheaper in Asian markets). They all freeze well and can be stored

in the freezer for up to 1 month. To use, defrost at room temperature for 45 minutes to 1 hour. If you can't find the size specified in a recipe, you can always buy a larger size and cut them down.

# GRILLED MEATBALL SKEWERS

*Look Chin Ping*

SPICE LEVEL: NONE

PREP TIME: 5 MINUTES · COOK TIME: 5 MINUTES

GLUTEN-FREE · SOY-FREE

This popular street-food snack is a super quick-and-easy addition to any backyard cookout. If you're making Chicken Satay Skewers (page 45), then it's easy to add these to the grill at the same time for more variety. The recipe uses Vietnamese-style beef meatballs, which are firm, bouncy, and a bit chewy—their texture is similar to the "snap" of good hot dogs. Look for them in Vietnamese, Chinese, or Thai grocery stores in the refrigerated or frozen section—they are sold in clear plastic packs and come in either smooth or "bumpy" varieties; you can use either for this recipe.

**SERVES 4 (2 SKEWERS PER PERSON)**

32 store-bought Vietnamese-style beef
meatballs (bò viên)

1. Prepare a charcoal or gas grill, hibachi, or stovetop grill pan.

2. Arrange 4 meatballs each on 8 (8-inch) bamboo skewers.

3. Grill on the charcoal or gas grill, hibachi, or on a stovetop grill pan until browned, turning frequently to brown evenly on all sides, about 5 minutes total. Be careful not to overcook them, as they are already cooked and just need to be heated through and browned.

**Recipe Tip:** *If using a charcoal grill, soak the bamboo skewers in cold water for 30 minutes before use to prevent them from catching fire on the grill.*

**Serving Suggestion:** *Serve with Sriracha sauce, hoisin sauce, and/or Sweet Chili Sauce (page 239 or store-bought) topped with finely chopped roasted peanuts and coarsely chopped fresh cilantro, for dipping.*

# FRIED TOFU

## *Taohu Tod*

SPICE LEVEL: NONE

PREP TIME: 5 MINUTES · COOK TIME: 5 MINUTES

GLUTEN-FREE · VEGAN

Every time I hear someone say they hate tofu, I think to myself, "Bet you haven't had good tofu!" Even the biggest skeptics might be converted into tofu lovers by this simple but delicious appetizer. The key is to get the tofu as dry as possible before frying, so that it will develop a crisp, golden-brown, nutty exterior around a soft, creamy interior. **MAKES 16 PIECES**

1 (17-ounce) block firm tofu (silken or plain, but plain firm tofu works better for frying)

Salt

Neutral oil, such as peanut or refined coconut oil, for frying

1. Slice the tofu in half lengthwise to create two thinner rectangles. Cut each half into quarters, and then cut each quarter diagonally to form small triangles. You should have 16 triangles.

2. Line a baking sheet with 4 layers of paper towels, and arrange the tofu triangles in a single layer on top of the paper towels. Lightly sprinkle the tofu with salt. Cover with 4 more layers of paper towels, and press gently but firmly all over to extract as much water as possible. (I like to then wrap each triangle in another paper towel and gently squeeze in order to dry the sides as well, just before frying.)

3. In a wok or large cast-iron skillet over medium-high heat, heat ½ inch of oil to 375°F (or until a cube of bread browns in the oil in about 30 seconds).

4. Fry the tofu triangles, being careful not to overcrowd them, turning them often with bamboo or wooden chopsticks or tongs to allow them to brown evenly on all sides until light golden brown, about 4 minutes total.

5.  Drain well on a paper towel-lined plate. Be careful not to overcook or the triangles will get dry and rubbery.

6.  Serve immediately; these are best when piping hot.

**Serving Suggestion:** *Serve with Sweet Chili Sauce (page 239 or store-bought) topped with finely chopped roasted peanuts and chopped fresh cilantro, for dipping. Though it's not traditional, they're also great dipped in Satay Peanut Sauce (page 243).*

**Leftover Tip:** *If you have any left over, you can use them as a vegetarian swap for the protein in any of the stir-fry or curry recipes in this book, or slice them up and use them as a filling for Fried Spring Rolls (page 34) or Fresh Spring Rolls (page 37).*

# FRIED SPRING ROLLS

## Poh Piah Tod

SPICE LEVEL: NONE

PREP TIME: 15 MINUTES · COOK TIME: 15 MINUTES

Though this popular starter is Chinese in origin, the ingredients in this version, as well as the smaller size, make it uniquely Thai. A street-food favorite, fried spring rolls can be made vegetarian by omitting the ground meat or replacing it with chopped or thinly sliced tofu. Spring rolls are a great way to use up leftover stir-fries or noodles—simply use them as the filling, following the same rolling and cooking instructions. **MAKES ABOUT 32 (3-INCH) ROLLS**

**FOR THE FILLING**

4 ounces bean thread noodles, soaked in warm water for 10 minutes to soften

2 ounces dried wood ear or shiitake mushrooms, soaked in warm water for 10 minutes to soften, then drained and thinly sliced (optional)

1 teaspoon whole white peppercorns

1 tablespoon chopped cilantro root or stems

1 tablespoon chopped garlic

1½ cups (10.6 ounces) ground pork or chicken

1 tablespoon vegetable oil

1 cup julienned or grated carrot

1 tablespoon fish sauce

**FOR THE ROLLS**

32 (5-inch square) spring roll wrappers, defrosted (if frozen) at room temperature for 45 minutes

Neutral oil, such as peanut or refined coconut oil, for frying

**TO MAKE THE FILLING**

1. Drain the soaked noodles, cut into 1-inch pieces, and set aside.

2. Drain the soaked mushrooms (if using), cut into thin slices, and set aside.

3. In a mortar and pestle (or spice grinder), crush the peppercorns to a fine powder.

4. Add the cilantro root to the mortar, and pound to form a paste.

5. Add the garlic and pound again to incorporate it into the paste. (If you don't have a mortar and pestle, then mince the garlic and cilantro root finely and

crush with the flat side of a chef's knife before mixing with the ground pepper in a small bowl.)

6. In a medium bowl, mix the paste thoroughly with the ground meat until evenly distributed.

7. In a large skillet over medium-low heat, heat the oil. Add the ground meat, raise the heat to medium, and stir-fry until browned, 6 to 7 minutes.

8. Add the carrot, noodles, mushrooms (if using), and fish sauce, and continue to stir-fry until the noodles and carrot have softened and turned translucent, 2 to 3 minutes. Remove the filling from the heat and let cool completely before rolling.

### TO MAKE THE ROLLS

1. Place the spring roll wrappers on a plate, and keep the unused stack covered with a damp, clean kitchen cloth to prevent them from drying out while you work. Keep a small bowl of water nearby for sealing the rolls.

2. On a flat work surface, place a wrapper with one of the corners pointing toward you.

3. Place 1 heaping tablespoon of the cooled filling just below the center of the wrapper.

4. Pull the corner pointing to you up and over the filling, tuck it under the filling, and roll up tightly, halfway.

5. Fold in the left and right sides to form an "envelope" shape (making sure the sides are perfectly straight and vertical) and continue rolling up, making sure the wrapper is tight around the filling, with no large air pockets.

6. When you've nearly reached the top, moisten the remaining corner with water using a pastry brush or your fingertip, finish rolling, and press down on the point to seal it.

*continued*

7.  Arrange the rolls, sealed-side-down, in a single layer on a baking sheet as you complete them. There's no need to keep the finished rolls covered, as letting them dry out a bit before frying will help them brown better.

8.  In a wok or large cast-iron skillet over medium-high heat, heat ½ inch of oil to 375°F (or until a cube of bread browns in the oil in about 30 seconds).

9.  Fry the rolls, being careful not to overcrowd them, turning them often with bamboo or wooden chopsticks or tongs to allow them to brown evenly on all sides until golden brown, 2 to 3 minutes total.

10. Drain well on a paper towel–lined plate and serve immediately.

**Serving Suggestion:** *Serve with Sweet Chili Sauce (page 239 or store-bought) topped with finely chopped roasted peanuts and chopped fresh cilantro, for dipping. Lettuce leaves and fresh mint leaves can also be served with the rolls, to wrap around each roll before eating.*

**Cooking Tip:** *Instead of frying, you can bake the rolls on a nonstick baking sheet at 375°F until crisp and browned, 10 to 15 minutes, turning halfway through to brown them evenly. They will not be as crisp or golden brown as fried spring rolls.*

**Ingredient Tip:** *You can also use ½ cup of any finely chopped fresh mushroom in place of the dried mushrooms.*

**Make-Ahead Tip:** *You can make the rolls and then freeze them before frying, wrapped tightly in plastic wrap, for up to 6 months. They can be fried directly while still frozen (add a few minutes to the cooking time).*

# FRESH SPRING ROLLS

*Poh Piah Sod*

SPICE LEVEL: NONE

PREP TIME: 15 MINUTES · COOK TIME: 10 MINUTES

GLUTEN-FREE

These crisp, refreshing, no-cook rolls (sometimes called "Summer Rolls") originate in Vietnam and are easy and fun to make. Optional additions include thinly sliced roast pork or thin slices of Chinese sausage (a thin, dried, ready-to-eat reddish sausage sold in Asian markets). They are great for picnics and backyard cookouts. **MAKES 8 ROLLS**

3 ounces thin rice-vermicelli noodles (makes about 2 cups noodles when softened)

8 (8-inch diameter) round, dried rice paper spring roll sheets

8 cooked shrimp, peeled and halved lengthwise

½ cup grated carrot

½ cup bean sprouts

¼ cup fresh mint leaves

¼ cup fresh cilantro leaves

2 or 3 scallions, green parts only, trimmed and cut into 4-inch lengths

1. In a small pot, bring enough water to cover the vermicelli noodles to a boil over high heat. Plunge the noodles into the boiling water to cover; take them off the heat and let them sit until softened, 6 to 8 minutes. Rinse them well in cold running water and set aside.

2. Arrange all ingredients in small bowls around your work area.

3. Fill a shallow pan or tray with very hot water.

4. Dip each rice paper sheet into the hot water and turn it in a circular motion with your fingers until it softens, 20 to 30 seconds. Gently shake off any excess water and place the softened rice sheet on a large plate or tray.

5. Place 2 shrimp halves, pink-side down, in the middle of the lower third of the sheet.

6. Arrange about ¼ cup of the vermicelli noodles in a cylindrical shape on top of the shrimp.

*continued*

7. Top the noodles with a little bit of the carrot and bean sprouts, then 3 or 4 mint leaves and 3 or 4 cilantro leaves and then one of the scallion sections.

8. Roll the rice sheet from the bottom up, tucking it tightly around the filling.

9. When halfway rolled, firmly fold in the left and right sides of the sheet to form an envelope shape.

10. Continue rolling and then place the finished roll, seam-side down, on a tray.

11. Let the rolls sit to dry for about 5 to 10 minutes before serving. They will keep for several hours at room temperature, wrapped in plastic wrap. They don't refrigerate well, however, because the wrappers and noodles will quickly become stiff and brittle.

**Serving Suggestion:** *Serve with 4 tablespoons Sweet Chili Sauce (page 239 or store-bought) thinned with 2 tablespoons fish sauce, sprinkled with finely chopped roasted peanuts and coarsely chopped fresh cilantro leaves, for dipping.*

**Simple Swaps:** *For a vegetarian or vegan version, simply omit the shrimp or replace it with 8 thin slices (½ inch wide, 3 inches long, and ¼ inch thick) of five-spice tofu or any other type of firm tofu.*

# NORTHERN THAI PORK AND TOMATO DIP

*Nam Prik Ong*

SPICE LEVEL: MILD

PREP TIME: 10 MINUTES, PLUS 15 MINUTES TO SOAK · COOK TIME: 30 MINUTES

NUT-FREE

This tasty, mild dip is a favorite in Northern Thailand, particularly in Chiang Mai. It is served as an appetizer or snack with steamed Sticky Rice (page 55), raw or lightly steamed vegetables, and crisp-fried pork rinds. Thai pork rinds are unseasoned, but you can use any kind of pork rind. **MAKES ABOUT 2 CUPS OR 4 TO 6 SERVINGS**

**FOR THE DIP PASTE**

4 or 5 dried Thai long chiles or any other 2- to 3-inch-long dried chiles, stemmed and seeded

½ teaspoon salt

½ cup thinly sliced shallots (about 3)

¼ cup thinly sliced garlic (about 4 cloves)

4 cilantro roots (or 1 tablespoon chopped cilantro stem, cut from the bottom inch)

1 tablespoon Thai fermented soybean/yellow bean sauce (see page 15; optional)

12 cherry tomatoes (about ½ pound), halved

1 teaspoon tamarind paste (see page 26 or store-bought; optional)

**FOR THE SAUCE**

4 tablespoons vegetable oil (or Fried Garlic in Oil, page 234)

1 tablespoon minced garlic (about 3 cloves)

2 tablespoons tomato paste

1 cup ground pork

12 cherry tomatoes (about ½ pound), quartered

1 teaspoon palm sugar or light brown sugar

1 teaspoon fish sauce

**FOR THE GARNISH**

1 tablespoon chopped fresh cilantro

1 tablespoon finely chopped scallion

**TO MAKE THE DIP PASTE**

1. In a small bowl of hot water, soak the dried chiles for 10 to 15 minutes, or until softened. Drain them well and chop coarsely.

*continued*

2. In a mortar and pestle, pound the chiles together with the salt, and then add the remaining paste ingredients, one at a time, pounding after each addition to form a coarse paste (or grind all paste ingredients together in a blender or food processor).

### TO MAKE THE SAUCE

1. In a large skillet over medium heat, heat the oil. Add the garlic and fry just until golden, 1 to 2 minutes.

2. Add the tomato paste, and cook until thickened and darkened, 1 to 2 minutes.

3. Add the dip paste, and cook until fragrant and slightly thickened, 2 to 3 minutes.

4. Add the ground pork, and cook, stirring frequently, until browned, about 5 minutes.

5. Stir in the cherry tomatoes, palm sugar, and fish sauce, and continue cooking, stirring occasionally, until the tomatoes have almost completely broken down, 10 to 15 minutes.

6. Remove from the heat, let cool, and serve slightly warm or at room temperature, topped with the chopped cilantro and scallions.

**Serving Suggestions:** *Traditionally this is served as a dipping sauce with crispy pork rinds and an assortment of raw or steamed vegetables, such as cucumber, string beans, and cabbage. You could also make a Thai-style pasta alla bolognese by serving it tossed with somen noodles (khanom jeen) or fresh egg noodles (bamee).*

# FISH CAKES

*Tod Mun Pla*

SPICE LEVEL: MILD

PREP TIME: 10 MINUTES · COOK TIME: 15 TO 20 MINUTES

GLUTEN-FREE · SOY-FREE · NUT-FREE

These firm, chewy cakes, fried till crisp and brown, don't taste much like fish but of fragrant red curry and kaffir lime. I enjoyed them for years as a child before ever realizing they were made from fish. Ground fish paste is often sold in Thai or Vietnamese markets in either the refrigerated or frozen section (it's okay if the paste has ingredients besides ground fish, as long as it's unseasoned), but you can also grind your own in a food processor or blender from the boneless filets of any firm white fish. Salmon and peeled shrimp also work. **MAKES ABOUT 24 CAKES**

4 kaffir lime leaves (2 double leaves)

1 pound ground fish paste or ground shrimp paste (don't confuse it with fermented fish paste or fermented shrimp paste, sold unrefrigerated in glass jars) or firm white fish (such as cod, catfish, or haddock)

¼ cup Red Curry Paste (page 130 or store-bought)

1 egg white

1 tablespoon fish sauce

1 cup thinly sliced (crosswise) Chinese long beans or green beans (about 12)

Neutral oil, such as peanut or refined coconut oil, for frying

Jasmine Rice (page 53), for serving

Ajaat (Cucumber Relish, page 242), for serving

1. Chiffonade the kaffir lime leaves: Stack the leaves on top of each other, roll them up tightly, and then slice as thinly as possible. They should yield about 2 teaspoons thinly sliced leaf. Set aside.

2. If you're using premade fish or shrimp paste, proceed to step 3. If you're making your own, trim all skin and bones away from the fish and puree in a food processor until a completely smooth, fine paste is formed.

*continued*

3. Place the fish paste, curry paste, egg white, and fish sauce in a large bowl and mix with a handheld mixer, or mix in a food processor or stand mixer with the dough-kneading attachment on medium-high speed, until smooth, shiny, and thoroughly combined, 4 to 5 minutes.

4. Fold in the green beans and kaffir lime leaves.

5. Wet your hands with cold water (or grease them with vegetable oil). Using your fingers, use 1 tablespoon of the mixture to form a small patty about 2 to 3 inches in diameter and ¼ inch thick. Repeat with the remaining mixture. Keep wetting your hands as needed, as the mixture will be quite sticky.

6. In a wok or Dutch oven over medium-high heat, heat 2 inches of oil to 375°F (or until a cube of bread browns in the oil in about 30 seconds).

7. Fry the fish cakes, being careful not to overcrowd them, turning them once with wooden chopsticks or tongs, until crisp and caramel-brown, about 3 minutes total.

8. Transfer the cakes from the oil to drain on a paper towel–lined plate using a mesh or wire spider.

9. Serve hot, with Ajaat (Cucumber Relish, page 242) and Jasmine Rice (page 53).

**Spice Lovers:** These fish cakes are relatively mild. If you want to turn up the heat, serve them with Spicy Fish Sauce (page 233), Sweet Chili Sauce (page 239), or Sriracha sauce.

**Make-Ahead Tip:** You can prepare the paste-and-curry mixture ahead of time and keep it refrigerated for up to 24 hours before frying.

**Cooking Tip:** Instead of frying, you could shape the mixture into fish balls and cook them in any soup or curry.

# CRISPY WONTON-WRAPPED SHRIMP ROLLS

*Goong Gra Bok*

SPICE LEVEL: NONE

PREP TIME: 5 MINUTES · COOK TIME: 5 TO 10 MINUTES

SOY-FREE · NUT-FREE

Though incredibly quick and easy to make, these shrimp rolls make an impression. Traditionally the shrimp are marinated in an aromatic paste before rolling, but this shortcut version, which my mother often made as a last-minute appetizer for dinner parties, is much faster and still tasty. **MAKES ABOUT 30 PIECES**

30 wonton wrappers

1 pound peeled, deveined, tail-on raw shrimp (about 30)

Neutral oil, such as peanut or refined coconut oil, for frying

Sweet Chili Sauce (page 239 or store-bought)

1. Place the wrappers on a clean work surface. Using your fingers, straighten out each shrimp a bit, and place it at the edge of one of the wrappers, leaving the tail off the wrapper.

2. Bring the remaining wrapper all the way over to cover the shrimp. Then, using your thumbs, grab the edge on which the shrimp is lying and roll up to form a cylinder.

3. Wet the tip of a finger with water and dampen the inside of the wrapper to help form a seal.

4. In a deep skillet, wok, or Dutch oven over medium-high heat, heat 1 inch of oil to 375°F (or until a cube of bread browns in the oil in about 30 seconds).

*continued*

5. Fry the rolls in batches, being careful not to overcrowd them, just until crisp and golden brown, 1 to 2 minutes.

6. Drain well on paper towels and serve with the chili sauce for dipping.

**Make-Ahead Tip:** *The uncooked rolled shrimp can be frozen, tightly wrapped in plastic wrap, for several months and fried without defrosting first; just add a little extra time for frying.*

# CHICKEN SATAY SKEWERS

## Satay Gai

SPICE LEVEL: NONE

PREP TIME: 20 MINUTES, PLUS 30 MINUTES TO MARINATE · COOK TIME: 10 TO 15 MINUTES

GLUTEN-FREE · SOY-FREE

Though originally of Malaysian or Indonesian origin, grilled satay skewers have been part of Thai cuisine for a long time and are extremely popular as a restaurant starter. They are also wonderful for backyard cookouts, as they taste best when cooked on a charcoal grill and are easy and fun to eat with your hands. **MAKES ABOUT 24 SKEWERS OR 4 TO 6 SERVINGS**

1 pound boneless chicken (white or dark meat)

24 (8-inch) bamboo skewers, soaked in cold water for 30 minutes before use

**FOR THE MARINADE**

1 teaspoon coriander seeds

1 teaspoon cumin seeds

1 teaspoon finely diced galangal

1 teaspoon finely chopped lemongrass

1 teaspoon white peppercorns

1 cup coconut milk

2 teaspoons palm sugar or light brown sugar

2 teaspoons ground turmeric

2 teaspoons fish sauce

Slice the chicken into thin strips, about 1 inch wide, 3 to 4 inches long, and ¼ inch thick. Cut against the grain so the meat will be more tender and easier to eat. Set aside.

**TO MAKE THE MARINADE**

1. In a small, dry, heavy-bottomed saucepan or skillet over low heat, toast the coriander and cumin seeds until fragrant, about 1 minute. Remove from the heat and let cool completely.

2. Pound the galangal, lemongrass, coriander and cumin seeds, and white peppercorns together with a mortar and pestle or spice grinder until evenly ground.

3. Transfer to a small bowl, and whisk together with the coconut milk, sugar, turmeric, and fish sauce. Mix well until the sugar dissolves.

*continued*

TO MAKE THE SKEWERS

1. Place the chicken strips in a shallow container and cover evenly with the marinade, stirring to distribute it over all surfaces of the meat. Cover with plastic wrap and place in the refrigerator to marinate for at least 30 minutes (or up to overnight).

2. Prepare a charcoal grill or heat a gas grill to 400°F. Thread the marinated chicken onto the drained, soaked skewers. If you have smaller pieces of leftover chicken, you can thread them together onto a single skewer. Set any leftover marinade aside.

3. Grill the skewered chicken on the charcoal or gas grill, or on a stovetop grill pan over medium-high heat, or under a broiler, turning to cook evenly on both sides and basting with the remaining marinade, as needed. Cook until cooked through, opaque, and with grill marks on each side, 4 to 6 minutes, making sure not to overcook the meat, and serve.

**Recipe Tip:** *The turmeric colors the chicken a bright yellow but can also stain your hands and fingernails; wear disposable rubber gloves when threading the skewers if you want to avoid that.*

**Serving Suggestion:** *Serve with Ajaat (Cucumber Relish, page 242) and slightly warm Satay Peanut Sauce (page 243). Satay skewers are typically also served with grilled or toasted pieces of white sandwich bread, which are dipped into the peanut sauce. Usually the tips of the skewers are used to spear the cucumber relish and the pieces of bread as well, so that no cutlery is required.*

**Simple Swaps:** *You can use an equal amount of beef, pork, or tofu in place of the chicken.*

# "CURRY PUFFS": THAI-STYLE CHICKEN-AND-POTATO SAMOSAS

### Gareepup

SPICE LEVEL: NONE

PREP TIME: 20 MINUTES · COOK TIME: 15 TO 20 MINUTES

NUT-FREE

This is a popular street-food snack, most likely of Indian origin. The original puff-pastry version requires two different kinds of dough and a complicated rolling process; this simplified version uses spring roll wrappers for a shortcut but is just as tasty. **MAKES ABOUT 30 PIECES**

**FOR THE FILLING**

1 tablespoon vegetable oil

1 garlic clove, minced

1½ teaspoons minced cilantro root or stem

½ cup finely diced onion

½ pound (8 ounces) chicken breast, finely diced, or coarsely ground chicken

1 large potato (about ½ pound), peeled and finely diced into ¼-inch cubes

1 tablespoon curry powder

1½ teaspoons soy sauce

1 teaspoon fish sauce or salt

1 teaspoon palm sugar, light brown sugar, or granulated white sugar

½ teaspoon ground white pepper

Water or broth, if needed

Salt, if needed

**FOR THE CURRY PUFFS**

30 sheets (3-by-10-inch) samosa wrappers; or 8 (10-inch square) spring roll wrappers, cut into 4 equal strips each; or 10 (8-inch square) spring roll wrappers, cut into 3 equal strips each

1 tablespoon all-purpose flour whisked into 1 tablespoon water (for sealing)

Neutral oil, such as peanut or refined coconut oil, for frying

*continued*

### TO MAKE THE FILLING

1. In a medium skillet over medium heat, heat the oil. Add the garlic and cilantro root or stem, and sauté until just fragrant, about 30 seconds.

2. Add the onion and continue sautéing until softened and transparent, about 1 minute.

3. Add the chicken and continue cooking just until browned, 2 to 3 minutes.

4. Add the potato, curry powder, soy sauce, fish sauce, sugar, and white pepper, and continue to cook, stirring frequently with a wooden spatula, until the potato is softened, 4 to 5 minutes. Add a little water or broth during cooking, if necessary, if the filling gets too dry and starts to stick to the bottom of the skillet.

5. Remove from the heat and set aside to cool completely to room temperature. When the filling has cooled completely, taste it and adjust the seasoning with salt, as necessary.

### TO MAKE THE CURRY PUFFS

1. Place a pastry sheet on a clean countertop with a long side facing you. Bring the top right corner down toward you and over the long edge close to you until a diamond with equal sides forms. The top corner of the created diamond should be at about the one-third point of the pastry.

2. Gently pat down along the fold, and then bring the fold up and over to the upper long edge farthest from you, lining it up with the straight edge of the pastry. This will form a small triangular pocket with a small flap (the remaining pastry length) to fold over the filling.

3. Fill the pocket with about 1 tablespoon of the cooled filling.

4. Dip a fingertip in the flour-water slurry and dampen the last pastry edge. Fold the remaining edge over the top of the pocket and press down gently to seal it shut.

5. In a deep skillet, wok, or Dutch oven over medium heat, heat 1 inch of oil to 350°F. Fry the curry puffs until golden brown, 2 to 3 minutes.

6. Drain well on paper towels and serve.

**Simple Swaps:** You can use ground turkey, beef, pork, or crumbled firm tofu or tempeh in place of the chicken.

**Cooking Tip:** Instead of frying, you can brush the puffs with vegetable oil or a lightly beaten egg and bake them in a 425°F oven until crisp and browned, about 20 minutes, turning them halfway through. (They will not be as brown or crisp as fried curry puffs.)

**Make-Ahead Tip:** You can freeze the folded uncooked curry puffs: Place them on a cookie sheet (not touching each other) and freeze. Once frozen, tightly wrap them together in plastic wrap and transfer to a resealable freezer bag. They can be frozen for several months. Cook directly from the freezer without defrosting, increasing cooking time as necessary.

# CHAPTER THREE

# Rice and Noodles

Rice is eaten in large quantities at nearly every Thai meal, and Thai dishes in general are heavily flavored and seasoned because they are intended to be eaten with generous amounts of rice. Fried rice, on the other hand, is intended as a one-dish meal.

Stir-fried rice noodles or noodle soups are also generally eaten as quick one-dish meals, rather than as part of a larger family style meal. Egg noodles (bamee) are also popular and can successfully be used in place of rice noodles in many stir-fry dishes and noodle soups.

The stir-fry recipes in this chapter yield about 2 servings; that's because making more than that at a time does not give good results—it will be difficult to stir-fry all the ingredients quickly enough to prevent burning and sticking, rice and noodles might get mushy and stick together, and you won't get the proper searing and browning. It's best, therefore, to stir-fry in batches of 1 to 2 servings at a time.

# Pad Thai

Probably the most internationally famous and popular Thai dish of all, Pad Thai (meaning "Thai-style stir-fry") has come to symbolize Thai cuisine around the world.

I must say that it has always puzzled me, and many Thais that I know, that it has become the most well-known Thai dish and the one by which many judge Thai restaurants. Though it is certainly delicious and complex when well made, it's not what I would choose as the most emblematic Thai dish, and in Thailand it is just one noodle dish among many—and more of a street food than a sit down–restaurant specialty.

It is, however, a good example of how Thai cuisine balances flavors—in this case, sweet, sour, and salty (the dish is typically not spicy at all, perhaps another reason it has gained so much international popularity)—and textures: soft noodles, chewy dried shrimp, and pickled radish offset by crunchy bean sprouts and peanuts. It's also another great testament to the ingenuity and adaptability of Thai cooks and the way they incorporate foreign dishes and cooking methods seamlessly into Thai cuisine.

While it's not clear who invented the dish, Prime Minister Phibunsongkhram popularized the dish back in the late 1930s and early 1940s, primarily as a means to reinforce Thai culture and identity (though rice noodles and the stir-frying technique are Chinese, other ingredients, such as tamarind and fish sauce, are distinctly Thai), stimulate the economy, and promote nutrition and food safety. The Thai government distributed the recipe for Pad Thai and encouraged street vendors to make it.

Traditional Pad Thai was intended as a showcase for uniquely Thai ingredients, so the original recipe does not include things like soy sauce, tomato paste, or ketchup. It should, therefore, be a light tan in color, not red or pink. That said, today many do add nontraditional ingredients, so feel free to add them if that's the style you prefer.

# JASMINE RICE

### *Khao Suay*

SPICE LEVEL: NONE

PREP TIME: 5 MINUTES · COOK TIME: 10 TO 20 MINUTES

GLUTEN-FREE · SOY-FREE · NUT-FREE · VEGAN

Some might think cooking plain rice too basic an operation to require much explanation, but I have seen some horrible things done to rice. Regardless of what package instructions or well-meaning friends might tell you, Asian rice should not be cooked like pasta—boiled vigorously in a large amount of salted water and then drained when it reaches an al dente consistency. Also, imported Thai jasmine rice—the best kind to use for Thai meals—requires a different rice-to-water ratio than other types of rice (see Recipe Tip). **SERVES 4 (MAKES ABOUT 6 CUPS COOKED RICE)**

2 cups uncooked jasmine rice (preferably from Thailand)

3 cups water (see Recipe Tip)

1. Rinse the rice well (see Note).

2. Transfer the rice to a medium pot, add the water, stir once or twice, bring to a boil over medium heat, and cover, reduce the heat to very low (the water should be at just a bare simmer), and simmer, undisturbed, until the water is absorbed, generally 10 to 12 minutes for new-crop rice (new-crop rice, generally labeled as such, has a higher moisture content), 15 to 20 minutes for old-crop (any rice not labeled as "new crop" can be assumed to be old-crop). Don't open the pot or stir the rice while it's cooking.

3. Remove from the heat and let rest, covered, 5 to 10 minutes. Fluff the rice with a fork or thin spatula before serving.

*continued*

**Note:** *Rinsing the rice gets rid of excess starch so that it will cook up light and fluffy rather than sticky and clumped together; this is especially important for rice that will be used to make fried rice, though to be honest I sometimes skip rinsing when I'm in a rush and making it to eat with, for example, a curry. There are several methods: Some place the rice in a fine-mesh strainer and rinse it in the sink under cold running water until the water runs clear; some place it in a large bowl (or the cooking pot) with enough water to cover, swish with their hands until the water is cloudy, carefully pour out the water, and then repeat 2 to 5 times. To avoid accidentally pouring rice down the drain, you can hold a splatter guard or inverted fine-mesh strainer over the top of the bowl or pot as you pour.*

**Recipe Tip:** *For the added water, it's difficult to give a one-size-fits-all prescription; you'll need to experiment a bit, since it will depend on the brand, whether the rice is new-crop or old-crop, and other factors, but in general, figure about 1¼ to 1½ cups water per 1 cup rice, and ½ cup uncooked rice per person. New-crop rice requires a bit less water, usually 1¼ cups water to 1 cup rice. Use a 1:1 ratio if making rice specifically for making fried rice the same day. Some don't measure but use the old-school method of cooking rice in enough water to cover by approximately one inch (equal to one fingertip), but I don't find that to be reliable.*

**Leftover Tip:** *The best way to reheat leftover rice is to sprinkle it with a bit of water and heat it in a microwave on high for about 2 minutes. The most obvious way to use up leftover rice is to use it to make fried rice, which, in fact, is best when made with leftover rice from the day before. You can also use it to make Quick Congee Rice Porridge (page 62) or Khao Tom rice soup (page 60).*

# STICKY RICE

*Khao Niew*

SPICE LEVEL: NONE

PREP TIME: 5 MINUTES, PLUS 4 HOURS TO SOAK · COOK TIME: 30 MINUTES

GLUTEN-FREE · SOY-FREE · NUT-FREE · VEGAN

This is the staple of northern and northeastern Thailand, traditionally steamed in large, cone-shaped bamboo baskets inserted in an urn-shaped metal pot, then served in small woven bamboo baskets with lids. It's typically eaten with your hands: Diners pinch off a small chunk, form it into a ball, and then dip it in sauces or use it to pick up some Lahb (page 110), Green Papaya Salad (page 99), etc. Be sure to use Thai sticky rice, not Japanese or any other kind, which cooks differently. Sometimes it's labeled "glutinous rice" (which just means it's sticky, not that it contains gluten). While steaming it in bamboo gives it a wonderful toasty, nutty scent, the traditional bamboo steamer is large and unwieldy. Suggestions are given for alternative methods. Some have had success cooking sticky rice in microwave ovens, but because microwaves vary widely in power, steaming is more universally reliable. SERVES 4

1¼ cups uncooked Thai sticky rice
(glutinous rice)

**TO STEAM USING A FINE-MESH STRAINER**

1. In a large bowl, soak the rice in enough cold water to cover for at least 4 hours and up to overnight. Drain.

2. In a large pot over medium heat, bring about 2 inches of water to a boil.

3. Place the rice in the fine-mesh strainer (with a lip or hooks that support it on the edge of the pot), place the strainer in the pot over the water, and cover. The water should not be touching the bottom of the rice.

*continued*

4. Adjust the heat so that the water is at a steady but gentle boil and steam, covered, until the rice is softened, translucent, and sticks together in lumps when pressed, 25 to 30 minutes. It should not be mushy. Flip the rice halfway through cooking using a rubber spatula.

5. Let sit, covered, for 10 to 15 minutes before serving. Keep covered with a damp cloth, or wrapped in plastic wrap, to prevent it from drying out if it will sit for a bit before serving.

## TO STEAM IN A STACKING METAL OR BAMBOO STEAMER

1. In a large bowl, soak the rice in enough cold water to cover for at least 4 hours and up to overnight. Drain well.

2. Add about 2 inches of water to a metal steamer, or enough water to a large pot under the bamboo steamer so that the top of the water will be about 2 to 3 inches below the rice.

3. Line the metal or bamboo steamer basket with a piece of cheesecloth or muslin, and place the rice in the center in an even layer. Fold the edges of the cloth up around the mound to wrap it, and cover the steamer with a lid.

4. Bring the water to boil over medium heat. Adjust the heat so that the water is at a steady but gentle boil, and place the covered bamboo steamer on top of the pot or assemble and cover the metal steamer.

5. Steam until the rice is tender and chewy, slightly translucent, and sticks together easily when pressed, 25 to 30 minutes (up to 45 minutes in a bamboo steamer). It should not be mushy. Halfway through cooking, gently flip the bundle.

6. Let sit, covered, for 10 to 15 minutes before serving. Keep covered with a damp cloth before serving to prevent it from drying out.

**Note:** For the fine-mesh strainer method, some people use a fine-mesh splatter guard, intended for protecting from grease spatters, rested on top of a pot of boiling water and then covered with a pot lid or inverted metal bowl. Sticky rice cooked this way will steam a bit faster, in about 15 to 20 minutes, but I've found it a bit more awkward and messy than the strainer method. Feel free to try both methods and choose your favorite.

**Leftover Tip:** Leftover sticky rice can be refrigerated, tightly wrapped in plastic wrap, for up to 1 day, but it will quickly dry out and harden. It can be sprinkled with a small amount of water and reheated in a microwave for 1 to 2 minutes on high but must be eaten immediately.

# COCONUT RICE

## Khao Mun Gati

SPICE LEVEL: NONE

PREP TIME: 5 MINUTES · COOK TIME: 15 MINUTES

GLUTEN-FREE · SOY-FREE · NUT-FREE · VEGAN

This rich, creamy rice can be used in place of plain steamed rice for any meal. It's particularly good when paired with spicy dishes that don't contain coconut milk, such as Jungle Curry (page 138) or Spicy Red Curry Stir-Fried Scallops with Basil (page 180). Some recipes for this rice call for a lot of salt and sugar, but I prefer to keep it simple since it will be eaten with highly flavored Thai dishes. This rice is more prone to burning on the bottom than rice cooked in just water, so making it in a rice cooker is a bit more foolproof. **SERVES 4**

2 cups uncooked jasmine rice

1¾ cups water

1 cup coconut milk

½ teaspoon salt

1. Rinse the rice well (see Note).

2. In a medium pot over medium heat, heat the water, coconut milk, and salt until the salt dissolves.

3. Transfer the rice to the pot, stir a few times, and bring to a boil. Cover, reduce the heat to the lowest setting, and simmer, undisturbed, until most of the coconut milk is absorbed, about 15 minutes. Don't open the pot or stir the rice while it's cooking.

4. Remove from the heat, stir a few times with a fork or spatula to distribute any remaining unabsorbed liquid, and let rest, covered, for 5 to 10 minutes. Fluff the rice with a fork or flat spatula before serving.

**Note:** There are several methods for rinsing rice: Some place the rice in a fine-mesh strainer and rinse it in the sink under cold running water until the water runs clear; some place it a large bowl (or the cooking pot) with enough water to cover, swish with their hands until the water is cloudy, carefully pour out the water, and then repeat 2 to 5 times. To avoid accidentally pouring rice down the drain, you can hold a splatter guard or inverted fine-mesh strainer over the top of the bowl or pot as you pour.

## STIR-FRYING . . . WITHOUT STIRRING?

The stir-fry recipes in this book were all developed using a carbon-steel wok on a gas stove. If you are instead using a 14-inch skillet or an electric stove, you'll need to modify the times and methods slightly. Woks are made of much thinner metal than skillets, so they heat up and react to temperature changes much faster. Nearly constant stirring in a wok is necessary to avoid burning, since they are generally used over very high or medium-high heat. To approximate the type of searing and caramelization you get when stir-frying in a wok, with a skillet you'll need to do the opposite: Let the ingredients sit and sear for a bit, without stirring at all. When making stir-fried noodle dishes, you'll need to do this even when using a wok, since home burners do not have nearly the same power as professional burners. It might seem counterintuitive at first, but it's the best way to get restaurant-style results.

# RICE SOUP WITH PORK MEATBALLS

*Khao Tom Look Chin Moo Sup*

SPICE LEVEL: NONE

PREP TIME: 10 MINUTES · COOK TIME: ABOUT 5 MINUTES

NUT-FREE

*Khao tom* rice soup is a popular Thai breakfast and classic comfort food—when I'm sick with a cold, this is what I crave. It can either be made plain—simply left-over cooked rice simmered in water, a blank slate that you can garnish any way you want—or more like a soup, as in this version, which makes a great one-dish meal for any time of day. One of the best bowls of *khao tom* I've ever had remains sharply in my mind: at a roadside stall in a small Thai village, with clear broth, garlicky pork meatballs, and a liberal dosing of freshly ground black pepper. **SERVES 4**

## FOR THE MEATBALLS

½ pound ground pork

1 tablespoon cilantro root or stem, finely chopped

1 tablespoon finely minced garlic (about 1 large clove)

2 teaspoons soy sauce

2 teaspoons fish sauce

1 egg white

¼ teaspoon ground white pepper

## FOR THE SOUP

6 cups unsalted Basic Thai Chicken Stock (page 91 or store-bought)

4 teaspoons soy sauce, Golden Mountain sauce, or Maggi seasoning sauce

4 teaspoons fish sauce

2 cups cooked jasmine rice (preferably day-old)

¼ cup thinly sliced Chinese celery, or the leaves and thin stems from the tops of regular celery stalks (optional)

¼ cup fresh cilantro, coarsely chopped

¼ cup Fried Garlic in Oil (page 234)

3 scallions, cut crosswise into ¼-inch slices

Freshly ground black pepper

In a medium bowl, mix well to combine all meatball ingredients. Set aside.

1. In a large stockpot over medium heat, bring the stock to a simmer.

2. Stir in the soy sauce and fish sauce.

3. Add the rice, and stir to separate any clumps.

4. Drop the meatball mixture by the scant tablespoonful into the soup (despite the name, there is no need to roll the meat into round balls; they are typically cooked in loose, irregular shapes). Simmer until the meatballs are cooked and the rice has softened a bit, about 3 minutes.

5. Top each serving with a sprinkling of celery (if using), cilantro, fried garlic and a bit of fried garlic oil, scallions, and a generous amount of freshly ground black pepper. Adjust the seasoning to taste, as necessary.

**Variations:** *To make plain rice soup, omit the meatballs and seasoning sauces and simmer the cooked rice in plain water or unsalted stock. Garnish with any of the suggested toppings or flavorings for Quick Congee Rice Porridge (page 62). Often khao tom or jok are made with bouncy pork meatballs (moo deng), rather than the looser, more crumbly ones in this recipe. For springy meatballs, process the meatball mixture in a food processor until it's smooth, sticky, and thoroughly combined, about 2 to 5 minutes, before using in this recipe.*

# QUICK CONGEE RICE PORRIDGE

### Jok

SPICE LEVEL: NONE

PREP TIME: 5 MINUTES, PLUS 10 MINUTES TO SOAK AND 4 HOURS TO FREEZE,
DEPENDING ON METHOD · COOK TIME: 10 TO 15 MINUTES, DEPENDING ON METHOD

GLUTEN-FREE · SOY-FREE · NUT-FREE · VEGAN

A Thai breakfast staple, *jok*, like Khao Tom rice soup (page 60), is great comfort food if you're feeling ill and can be topped with whatever you like. Normally it's made by either cooking broken jasmine rice (sold in Asian markets) in water or stock for at least one hour until it naturally breaks down into a porridge, or by simmering leftover rice or plain Rice Soup (Khao Tom, page 60) until the grains of rice break down, again for several hours. To get around such long cooking times, here are a couple of shortcut methods: using precooked rice and an immersion blender or using soaked uncooked rice that has been frozen. **SERVES 4 TO 5**

## METHOD 1

3 cups cooked jasmine rice

7 cups water or Basic Thai Chicken Stock
(if not vegetarian or vegan; page 91)

1. In a large stockpot over high heat, bring the rice and water to a boil.

2. Turn the heat to low and simmer, covered, until the rice gets very soft and starts to break down, 5 to 10 minutes.

3. Turn off the heat and blend with an immersion blender (or in a blender or food processor) just until it forms a coarse porridge with small pieces of rice still visible (no whole grains), about 1 minute. The congee will thicken a bit as it cools; if you prefer a thinner consistency, add some hot water.

## METHOD 2

⅔ cup uncooked jasmine rice

6 cups water or Basic Thai Chicken Stock (if not vegetarian or vegan; page 91)

1. In a small bowl, soak the rice in enough cold water to cover for 10 minutes.

2. Drain well and transfer the rice to a resealable freezer bag and freeze for at least 4 hours and up to overnight.

3. In a large stockpot over high heat, bring the water to a boil.

4. Add the frozen, uncooked rice and cook, uncovered, at a rapid boil, stirring frequently, until the rice grains break down and turn into congee, about 15 minutes. The congee will thicken as it cools; if you prefer a thinner consistency, add some hot water.

**Serving Suggestions:** In Thailand, jok is often eaten with chromosome-shaped savory donuts called patong goh, topped with julienned ginger (in very thin matchsticks) and chopped scallions and cilantro. Other optional flavorings and toppings include an egg dropped or stirred in just after turning off the heat, soy sauce, fish sauce, Maggi or Golden Mountain seasoning sauce (see page 16), freshly ground white or black pepper, Fried Garlic in Oil (page 234), Crispy Fried Shallots (page 235), Pickled Chiles in Vinegar (page 231), a Fried Egg (page 185), pieces of Thai-Style Omelet (page 187), chopped roasted peanuts, thinly sliced Chinese celery (or the leaves and thin stems of regular celery), pickled cabbage or radish, mustard greens, preserved radish (see page 16), "flossy pork" or moo yong (a Chinese shredded and fried pork with a texture resembling steel wool), kim chee, roast duck, Crispy Garlic-Pepper Pork (page 212), fried fish, shrimp, or any thinly sliced meat. Congee is a great way to use up leftover stir-fry too–just stir it in.

# FRIED RICE WITH PORK AND TOMATOES

## Khao Pad Moo

SPICE LEVEL: NONE

PREP TIME: 10 MINUTES · COOK TIME: 10 MINUTES

NUT-FREE

Fried rice might just be the best thing made from leftovers, and Thai-style fried rice will forever be my favorite kind. It's quick, kid-friendly, and easy to tailor to your tastes. Though you can skip the garnishes, to me they are what really make this one-dish meal special; the contrast of cool, crisp cucumber with the steaming-hot rice is indescribably perfect. **SERVES 2**

1 tablespoon soy sauce

2 teaspoons fish sauce

Pinch granulated sugar

2 tablespoons vegetable oil

1 tablespoon minced garlic (about 2 large cloves)

1 small onion, cut into ½-inch wedges

4 ounces boneless pork, cut into thin, bite-size pieces (about ¼ inch by 2 to 3 inches)

1 egg

2 cups cooked rice, at room temperature (preferably day-old)

3 scallions, cut into ¼-inch slices

1 tomato, cored and cut into wedges

8 thin (¼-inch) cucumber slices (see "Cutting Cucumbers," page 24, for extra-special presentation)

Pinch ground white pepper

2 tablespoons fresh cilantro leaves

2 lime wedges

1. In a small bowl, mix to combine the soy sauce, fish sauce, and sugar, and set aside.

2. In a wok or large skillet over medium heat, heat the oil. Add the garlic and stir-fry until fragrant, 30 seconds to 1 minute.

3. Add the onion and cook until softened and slightly browned, 1 to 2 minutes.

4. Add the pork and stir-fry just until no longer pink, 2 to 3 minutes.

5. Crack the egg into the center of the wok or skillet and cook it, stirring with a wooden spoon, until it starts to set, 30 seconds to 1 minute.

6. Add the rice and stir-fry until it is evenly mixed with the egg, about 1 minute.

7. Add the sauce mixture, scallions, and tomato, and stir-fry for 2 minutes longer.

8. Serve with the cucumber slices arranged in a fan shape on the plate, and sprinkle the rice with the pepper and cilantro leaves. Each diner can squeeze a lime wedge over their serving.

**Serving Suggestion:** *Serve with a small bowl of Spicy Fish Sauce (page 233) or Chiles in Lime Sauce (page 232).*

**Simple Swaps:** *In place of the pork, you can use any meat, seafood, tofu, vegetables, or leftover stir-fry.*

## RICE FOR FRIED RICE

It's best to use day-old, leftover, old-crop rice to make fried rice (rice labeled "new crop" has a higher moisture content and can get mushy when fried), but if you are boiling rice specifically to use in a fried rice recipe the same day, then use a bit less water than you normally would (use a 1:1 rice-to-water ratio) and be sure to rinse the rice well before cooking. You can spread cooked rice out on a plate and refrigerate it to cool it faster, but let it come to room temperature before use; otherwise it can get gummy and clump together when stir-fried.

# PINEAPPLE FRIED RICE WITH CURRY POWDER AND SHRIMP

## Khao Pad Supparote

SPICE LEVEL: NONE

PREP TIME: 10 MINUTES · COOK TIME: 5 MINUTES

Another childhood favorite, this is a dish I loved ordering in restaurants because it would often come served in half of a hollowed-out pineapple. That would be an impressive way to serve it for a dinner party, but this kid-friendly recipe is so quick and easy that it also makes a great weeknight one-dish meal. **SERVES 2**

1 tablespoon soy sauce

2 teaspoons fish sauce

2 teaspoons curry powder

Pinch granulated sugar

2 tablespoons vegetable oil

1 tablespoon minced garlic

¼ cup very thinly sliced onion

10 medium raw shrimp, peeled and deveined, tails left on

1 egg

2 cups cooked rice, at room temperature (preferably day-old)

1 cup 1-inch chunks fresh pineapple

½ cup roasted cashew nuts

2 scallions, cut into ¼-inch slices

2 tablespoons fresh cilantro leaves

2 lime wedges

1. In a small bowl, mix to combine the soy sauce, fish sauce, curry powder, and sugar, and set aside.

2. In a wok or large skillet over medium heat, heat the oil. Add the garlic and stir-fry until fragrant, 30 seconds to 1 minute.

3. Add the onion, and cook until fragrant and the onion is softened, about 30 seconds.

4. Add the shrimp, and stir-fry just until it starts to turn pink, about 1 minute.

5. Crack the egg into the center of the wok or skillet, and stir with a wooden spoon or spatula to mix the egg and yolk well, about 30 seconds.

6.  Add the rice, and stir-fry until it is evenly mixed with the egg, about 1 minute.

7.  Add the sauce mixture, pineapple, cashews, and scallions, and stir-fry for 30 seconds longer.

8.  Serve sprinkled with the cilantro and with the lime wedges, for squeezing over each portion.

**Simple Swaps:** You can use any thinly sliced meat or tofu in place of the shrimp.

# GREEN CURRY FRIED RICE

*Khao Pad Gaeng Kiew Wan*

SPICE LEVEL: MEDIUM

PREP TIME: 5 MINUTES · COOK TIME: 5 MINUTES

GLUTEN-FREE · NUT-FREE

This dish combines intense green curry flavors with the speed and ease of fried rice for a super-quick and satisfying one-dish meal. It's particularly tasty when made with homemade Green Curry Paste (page 132). You can use any type of curry paste this way, with any meat, seafood, tofu, or vegetables that you prefer. You can even stir-fry a few tablespoons of any leftover curry with several cups of leftover rice. **SERVES 2**

2 tablespoons vegetable oil

2 tablespoons Green Curry Paste (page 132 or store-bought)

1 tablespoon water, if needed

2 teaspoons fish sauce

1 teaspoon palm sugar or granulated sugar

4 ounces of any boneless meat (such as pork or chicken), cut against the grain into thin, bite-size pieces (about ¼ inch by 2 to 3 inches)

½ cup fresh or frozen green peas

2 cups cooked rice, at room temperature (preferably day-old)

2 fresh kaffir lime leaves, center ribs removed and julienned (optional)

1 cup fresh Thai sweet or Italian sweet basil leaves (optional)

1. In a wok or large skillet over medium heat, heat the oil. Add the curry paste and stir-fry until fragrant, about 1 minute.

2. Add the water (if needed), fish sauce, and sugar, and stir-fry until the sugar dissolves, about 30 seconds.

3. Add the meat and peas, and stir-fry until the meat is no longer pink, 3 to 4 minutes.

4. Add the rice and kaffir lime leaves (if using), and stir-fry for about 1 minute.

5. Turn off the heat, and stir in the basil leaves (if using) just until wilted. Serve immediately.

**Simple Swaps:** In place of the green peas, you can use any other finely diced vegetable.

# TOM YUM FRIED RICE WITH SHRIMP

## Khao Pad Tom Yum

SPICE LEVEL: MEDIUM

PREP TIME: 10 MINUTES · COOK TIME: 5 MINUTES

NUT-FREE

This dish combines the hot-and-sour flavors of popular Tom Yum Soup (page 93) with the speed and ease of stir-fried rice for a spicy, satisfying one-dish meal. If you're a fan of tom yum soup, you'll love this fried rice! The fresh galangal and kaffir lime leaves really give it an authentic flavor, but if you can't find them, you can omit them and just use lemongrass. **SERVES 2**

2 tablespoons finely sliced fresh or frozen lemongrass (from the bottom 3 inches of about 4 stalks; see "Using Lemongrass," page 120)

1 tablespoon finely chopped fresh or frozen galangal

1 small fresh or frozen kaffir lime leaf, central ribs removed and discarded, leaf very finely julienned

2 fresh red Thai chiles, stemmed and chopped

1 tablespoon fish sauce

1 tablespoon soy sauce

4 teaspoons Roasted Chili Paste (page 240 or store-bought)

1 tablespoon freshly squeezed lime juice

2 tablespoons vegetable oil

1 scallion, white part very thinly sliced crosswise, dark green part sliced crosswise into ¼-inch rings, kept separate

1 cup quartered small white or button mushrooms (or drained canned straw mushrooms, halved)

10 medium raw shrimp, peeled and deveined, tails left on

2½ cups cooked jasmine rice, at room temperature (preferably day-old)

1 small tomato, cored, seeded, and cut into wedges

¼ cup coarsely chopped fresh cilantro

Lime wedges, for serving

1. In a mortar and pestle or blender, pound or grind the lemongrass, galangal, kaffir lime leaves, and chiles together to form a coarse paste.

2. Transfer the paste to a small bowl, and stir in the fish sauce, soy sauce, chili paste, and lime juice. Set aside.

3. In a wok or large skillet over medium heat, heat the oil.

4. Add the scallion whites, mushrooms, and shrimp, and stir-fry for 1 minute.

5. Add the rice and sauce mixture, and stir just until all the ingredients are coated evenly with sauce. Use a wooden spoon or spatula to break up any large clumps of rice.

6. Add the tomato and scallion greens, and stir-fry for 1 minute more.

7. Turn off the heat, add the cilantro, stir to distribute evenly, and serve immediately, with lime wedges for squeezing on top.

**Simple Swaps:** *In place of the shrimp, you can use 4 ounces of any boneless meat (for example, pork or chicken), cut against the grain into thin, bite-size pieces (about ¼ inch by 2 to 3 inches).*

# PAD THAI

SPICE LEVEL: NONE

PREP TIME: 10 MINUTES · COOK TIME: 10 MINUTES

GLUTEN-FREE

If you make Pad Thai often, you can mix up a large batch of the sauce and keep it in the refrigerator to make prep even easier and faster. Unlike with the stir-fried fresh noodle dishes, charring is not desirable in Pad Thai, so it's generally cooked at a slightly lower heat and a bit more slowly. **SERVES 2**

4 ounces dried thin rice noodles (see Note 1)

¼ cup fish sauce

3 tablespoons palm sugar, light brown sugar, or granulated sugar

2 tablespoons tamarind paste (page 26 or store-bought)

3 tablespoons vegetable oil, divided

12 medium raw shrimp, peeled and deveined, tails left on

2 tablespoons minced shallot

1 tablespoon minced garlic

1 to 2 tablespoons water or broth, if needed

2 eggs

2 cups bean sprouts, divided

½ cup pressed tofu or bean curd (see Note 2), cut into ¼-inch by ¼-inch by 2-inch slices

3 scallions, green parts only, cut into 1½-inch lengths

¼ cup roasted peanuts (preferably unsalted), plus more for serving, slightly crushed in a mortar and pestle or roughly chopped

Lime wedges, for serving

1. Bring a large pot of water to boil over high heat. Once boiling, turn off the heat, add the noodles, stir a few times, and let sit for 5 minutes. Rinse the noodles well under cold water and drain well. Use your fingers to separate any stuck-together strands and set aside.

2. In a small bowl, mix to combine the fish sauce, palm sugar, and tamarind paste, and set aside.

3. In a wok or large skillet over medium heat, heat 1 tablespoon of oil.

4.  Add the shrimp and stir-fry just until pink and opaque, 2 to 3 minutes. Remove the shrimp from the wok or skillet with a mesh skimmer or slotted spoon and set aside.

5.  Heat the remaining 2 tablespoons oil in the wok or skillet, and add the shallot and garlic. Stir-fry until fragrant and slightly golden, 30 seconds to 1 minute.

6.  Add the noodles and sauce mixture, and stir-fry until well-combined and the noodles are soft, but not mushy, about 1 minute; add 1 to 2 tablespoons water or broth if the noodles are not soft enough.

7.  Push the noodles to the sides of the wok or skillet with a wooden spoon or spatula.

8.  Crack the eggs into the middle of the wok or skillet, and scramble with a wooden spoon just until nearly set, about 30 seconds.

9.  Add the cooked shrimp, 1 cup bean sprouts, and the tofu, scallions, and peanuts, and toss to combine.

10. Serve immediately, with the lime wedges, the remaining 1 cup bean sprouts, and additional peanuts to sprinkle on each serving, as desired.

**Note 1:** *Look for dried, flat rice noodles about ¼ inch wide. These are the same noodles used for Vietnamese pho noodle soup. Sometimes the package will read "Chantaboon (or Jantaboon) Rice Stick."*

**Note 2:** *Pressed tofu (or pressed bean curd) is sold in Asian markets in the refrigerated section in clear plastic packaging, not packed in water, and is sold in small, flat squares about ¼ to ½ inch thick. Sometimes it's yellow or brown in color, from being marinated in soy sauces or spices, and other times it is white. You can use any of those kinds in this recipe, or, if you can't find pressed tofu, use extra-firm tofu.*

*continued*

**Serving Suggestion:** Along with the lime wedges, serve with Ground Roasted Chili Powder (page 230), Pickled Chiles in Vinegar (page 231), granulated sugar, and fish sauce, for each diner to season their serving to taste.

**Variations:** You can use ⅓ cup small dried shrimp in place of the fresh shrimp and add 1 tablespoon finely chopped preserved salted radish (see page 16) for a more traditional version. You can add 4 ounces boneless, skinless chicken breast, cut against the grain into thin, bite-size pieces (about ¼ inch by 2 to 3 inches) in addition to, or in place of, the shrimp. For a vegetarian version, omit the chicken and shrimp and use soy sauce in place of the fish sauce.

## USING DRIED RICE NOODLES

Stir-fried noodle dishes such as Pad See Ew, Rad Na, and Pad Kee Mao are typically made with chewy fresh rice noodles, which will give the best results, but if you can't find them, you can substitute dried rice noodles, using the widest ones that you can find. Pad Thai, on the other hand, usually is made with thinner dried rice noodles, the same noodles used to make the Vietnamese noodle soup *pho*. Common Thai kitchen wisdom says that dried rice noodles should be soaked in room-temperature water for about 30 to 40 minutes before use in stir-frying, never hot water, and never boiled like pasta before use in a stir-fry, lest you wind up with a sticky, mushy, clumped-together mess. However, multiple tests failed to produce consistent results with dried noodles soaked in either room-temperature, warm, or hot tap water, and I was unable to come up with a soaking time that would work across brands and kitchens ("room-temperature" clearly means something different in Thailand than, say, Minnesota in the dead of winter). So, I've broken with tradition and recommended not boiling the dried noodles, which would indeed lead to sticky clumps, but soaking them briefly in boiled water, off-heat, then rinsing in abundant cold water, separating any strands that are stuck together with your fingers before use, just as you would with fresh rice noodles. Prepped this way, they cook quickly and consistently in stir-fry recipes, without clumping.

# STIR-FRIED RICE NOODLES
# WITH SOY SAUCE

*Pad See Ew*

SPICE LEVEL: NONE

PREP TIME: 10 MINUTES · COOK TIME: 10 MINUTES

NUT-FREE

It's a bit tricky to recreate restaurant- or street vendor-style stir-fried noodles at home—with a bit of char and smoky flavor—without a blazing professional burner, but it can be done; the key is to use high heat and stir less than you'd normally be inclined to (see "Stir-Frying . . . Without Stirring?" on page 59). If you're using a well-seasoned carbon-steel wok (see page 19), your noodles will taste even better. As with all stir-fries, it's important to have all ingredients prepped and ready to go, because everything happens very quickly once the wok is heated. **SERVES 2**

¾ pound (12 ounces) fresh 1-inch-wide rice noodles, or 7 ounces dried rice noodles

2 tablespoons water

½ teaspoon baking soda

6 ounces boneless pork (or any other meat), cut against the grain into thin, bite-size pieces (about ¼ inch by 2 to 3 inches)

2 tablespoons dark sweet soy sauce (aka "black sweet soy sauce"; see page 8)

1 tablespoon soy sauce

1 tablespoon fish sauce

2 teaspoons oyster sauce

2 tablespoons vegetable oil

1 tablespoon chopped garlic

1 egg

4 cups Chinese broccoli (choy sum or gai lan), broccoli, or broccolini, cut into 1- to 2-inch pieces, stems thinly sliced crosswise (about ¼ inch thick)

1. If using fresh noodles, unless the noodles are super-fresh and soft, you'll need to soften them a bit before use: Microwave them just until they are softened and separate easily (heat for 30 seconds at a time, checking after each increment to see if they are softened enough), 1 to 2 minutes. When cool enough to handle, separate them using your fingers and set aside.

*continued*

2. If you can't find fresh, purchase the widest dried rice noodles you can find. Bring a large pot of water to a boil, turn off the heat, add the dried noodles, stir a few times, and let them sit for about 8 minutes. Rinse well in cold water, drain well, separate any stuck-together strands using your fingers, and set aside.

3. In a medium bowl, mix to combine the water and baking soda. Add the meat, and toss to coat. Set aside for at least 5 minutes (and up to 15 minutes) to tenderize.

4. In a small bowl, mix to combine the soy sauces, fish sauce, and oyster sauce, and set aside.

5. When the meat is done tenderizing, rinse it well in running water and drain well.

6. In a large wok or skillet over medium-high heat, heat the oil. Add the garlic and stir-fry just until fragrant, 15 to 30 seconds.

7. Add the meat and stir-fry just until browned, about 2 minutes.

8. Crack the egg into the center and stir-fry for about 30 seconds.

9. Add the noodles, broccoli, and sauce mixture, and stir well until combined. (If using dried rice noodles, stir-fry until the noodles are softened, 1 to 2 minutes; if using fresh noodles, proceed directly to the next step.)

10. Let sit for about 1 minute, until the noodles are a bit charred, and then stir well, scraping the bottom of the wok or skillet with a wooden spoon or spatula to remove any stuck-on bits.

11. Flip the noodles with a wooden spatula and let sit on the other side for 1 minute longer; serve immediately.

**Ingredient Tip:** Dark sweet soy sauce (sometimes labeled as "black sweet soy sauce"; see page 8) is a very thick, dark, sweet-and-salty Thai soy sauce sold in Asian markets. If you can't find it, you can approximate it by mixing 1 tablespoon soy sauce with 1 tablespoon palm sugar or brown sugar and 1 teaspoon dark molasses. Use 2 tablespoons of the resulting mixture in place of the dark sweet soy sauce in this recipe.

**Recipe Tip:** The meat is briefly soaked in a water-baking soda solution to tenderize it to a silky texture (see "Velveting Meat for Tender Texture," page 204); you can skip this step if using seafood or tofu, or if you're short on time.

**Serving Suggestion:** This dish is typically served with Pickled Chiles in Vinegar (page 231) and sprinkled with ground white pepper. Other optional accompaniments (for each diner to sprinkle on top of their serving as desired) include Ground Roasted Chili Powder (page 230), Spicy Fish Sauce (page 233), granulated sugar, and Chiles in Lime Sauce (page 232).

# STIR-FRIED RICE NOODLES WITH GRAVY

## Rad Na

SPICE LEVEL: NONE

PREP TIME: 10 MINUTES · COOK TIME: 15 MINUTES

NUT-FREE

It would be difficult for me to name my favorite noodle dish, since I love noodles in any shape or form, but rad na is in my top five. It's similar to Pad See Ew (page 75) in that it uses the same chewy, smoky, wide rice noodles, but with a mild, savory gravy poured on top. My mom would always have a plate of it waiting for me when I came home to visit from college. The Thai name amused me when I was a kid—it translates literally as "poured on the face," referring, of course, to the gravy poured onto the noodles, but I'd always imagine someone having the sauce poured on their face and giggle. **SERVES 2**

¾ pound (12 ounces) fresh 1-inch-wide rice noodles, or 7 ounces dried rice noodles

2 tablespoons water

½ teaspoon baking soda

6 ounces flank steak (or any other meat), cut against the grain into thin, bite-size pieces (about ¼ inch by 2 to 3 inches)

2 tablespoons oyster sauce

2 tablespoons fermented soybean/yellow soybean sauce (see page 15)

1½ cups water or Basic Thai Chicken Stock (page 91)

1 tablespoon fish sauce

2 tablespoons cornstarch

¼ cup water

4 tablespoons vegetable oil, divided, plus 1 tablespoon more, if needed

2 tablespoons dark sweet soy sauce (aka "black sweet soy sauce"; see page 8)

1 tablespoon chopped garlic

4 cups Chinese broccoli (choy sum or gai lan), broccoli, or broccolini, cut into 1- to 2-inch pieces, stems thinly sliced crosswise (about ¼ inch thick)

1. If using fresh noodles, unless the noodles are super-fresh and soft, you'll need to soften them a bit before use: Microwave them just until they are softened and separate easily (heat for 30 seconds at a time, checking after each increment to see if they are softened enough), about 1 to 2 minutes. When cool enough to handle, separate them using your fingers and set aside.

2.  If you can't find fresh, purchase the widest dried rice noodles you can find. Bring a large pot of water to boil, turn off the heat, add the dried noodles, stir a few times, and let them sit for about 8 minutes. Rinse well in cold water, drain well, separate any stuck-together strands using your fingers, and set aside.

3.  In a medium bowl, mix to combine the water and baking soda. Add the meat, and toss to coat. Set aside for at least 5 minutes (and up to 15 minutes) to tenderize.

4.  In another medium bowl, mix to combine the oyster sauce, soybean sauce, water, and fish sauce, and set aside.

5.  In a small bowl, whisk the cornstarch into the water, and set aside.

6.  When the meat is done tenderizing, rinse it well in running water and drain well.

7.  In a large wok or skillet over medium-high heat, heat 2 tablespoons of the oil. Add the noodles and dark sweet soy sauce, and stir just until the noodles are evenly coated. Let the noodles sit for about 30 seconds to develop a bit of char, and then stir and let sit for about 30 seconds longer to char a bit more. You can add another tablespoon of oil to the pan if they are sticking too much. (If using dried rice noodles, use medium heat and stir-fry until softened, about 1 to 2 minutes, before letting sit to char a bit.)

8.  Transfer the noodles to a large bowl, and cover to keep warm.

9.  In the wok or skillet over medium heat, heat the remaining 2 tablespoons oil. Add the garlic, and stir-fry just until fragrant, 15 seconds to 30 seconds.

10.  Add the meat, and stir-fry just until browned, about 2 to 3 minutes.

11.  Add the broccoli, and stir-fry for about 1 minute.

12.  Add the sauce mixture, and bring to a simmer.

*continued*

13. Stir the cornstarch-water mixture to incorporate any cornstarch that has sunk to the bottom of the bowl, and add it to the wok or skillet.

14. Simmer until the sauce has thickened into a gravy-like consistency, 30 seconds to 1 minute.

15. Pour half of the gravy over each serving of noodles, and serve immediately.

**Ingredient Tip:** Dark sweet soy sauce (sometimes labeled as "black sweet soy sauce"; see page 8) is a very thick, dark, sweet-and-salty Thai soy sauce sold in Asian markets; if you can't find it, you can approximate it by mixing 1 tablespoon soy sauce with 1 tablespoon palm sugar or brown sugar and 1 teaspoon dark molasses; use 2 tablespoons of the resulting mixture in place of the dark sweet soy sauce in this recipe.

**Recipe Tip:** The meat is briefly soaked in a water-baking soda solution to tenderize it to a silky texture (see "Velveting Meat for Tender Texture," page 204); you can skip this step if using seafood or tofu, or if you're short on time.

**Serving Suggestion:** This dish is typically served with Pickled Chiles in Vinegar (page 231) and sprinkled with ground white pepper. Other optional accompaniments (for each diner to sprinkle on top of their serving as desired) include Ground Roasted Chili Powder (page 230), Spicy Fish Sauce (page 233), granulated sugar, and Chiles in Lime Sauce (page 232).

**Variations:** You can also make this dish with thin, fresh egg noodles—either deep-fried till crisp, stir-fried, or boiled and drained—with the gravy poured on top.

# SPICY DRUNKEN NOODLES

*Pad Kee Mao*

SPICE LEVEL: HOT

PREP TIME: 10 MINUTES · COOK TIME: 15 MINUTES

NUT-FREE

Allegedly the name of this dish (more accurately translated as "drunkard stir-fry") stems from the fact that some lushes love to eat spicy food during (or after) a late-night bender. It was originally a meat stir-fry that contained no noodles. It's typically made with peppery holy basil, but you can use any type of fresh basil. This recipe is quite spicy—reduce the number of chiles, seed them, or use jalapeños instead for a milder dish. **SERVES 2**

¾ pound (12 ounces) fresh 1-inch-wide rice noodles, or 6 ounces dried rice noodles

1 tablespoon dark sweet soy sauce (aka "black sweet soy sauce"; see page 8)

1 tablespoon soy sauce

1½ teaspoons oyster sauce

1½ teaspoons fish sauce

4 or 5 fresh red Thai bird's-eye, serrano, or jalapeño chiles, stemmed

1 tablespoon chopped garlic

2 tablespoons vegetable oil

½ onion, cut into ½-inch wedges

6 ounces boneless, skinless chicken breast (or any other meat), cut against the grain into thin, bite-size pieces (about ¼ inch by 2 to 3 inches)

1 tomato, cored and cut into wedges

2 stems of young green peppercorns, fresh or brined (optional but recommended)

1½ cups fresh holy basil, Thai sweet basil, or Italian sweet basil leaves

1. If using fresh noodles, unless the noodles are super-fresh and soft, you'll need to soften them a bit before use: Microwave them just until they are softened and separate easily (heat for 30 seconds at a time, checking after each increment to see if they are softened enough), about 1 to 2 minutes. When cool enough to handle, separate them using your fingers and set aside.

2. If you can't find fresh, purchase the widest dried rice noodles you can find. Bring a large pot of water to boil, turn off the heat, add the dried noodles, stir a few times, and let them sit for about 8 minutes. Rinse well in cold water, drain well, separate any stuck-together strands using your fingers, and set aside.

*continued*

3. In a small bowl, mix to combine the soy sauces, oyster sauce, and fish sauce, and set aside.

4. Slice 2 of the chiles lengthwise, seed them, and set them aside. Chop the remaining 2 or 3 chiles roughly.

5. In a mortar and pestle, pound the chopped chiles and garlic together to form a coarse paste (or mince them together finely with a chef's knife, and then mash them a bit with the flat side of the knife to form a coarse paste).

6. In a large wok or skillet over medium heat, heat the oil. Add the chile-garlic paste and stir-fry just until fragrant, 10 to 20 seconds.

7. Add the onion, and stir-fry until softened and a bit browned, 1 to 2 minutes.

8. Add the meat and stir-fry just until browned, 3 to 4 minutes.

9. Push everything to the sides of the wok or skillet with a wooden spoon or spatula. Add the noodles in the center, pour the sauce on top of the noodles, and stir a few times to distribute evenly.

10. Add the tomato and green peppercorn stems (if using) and sliced chiles, and stir a few times to mix well.

11. Cook until the noodles are softened and just a bit browned or charred: Let the noodles sit for about 1 minute, without stirring, and then mix and let sit for 1 minute more.

12. Turn off the heat, add the basil, and stir a few times just until the basil is softened. Serve immediately.

> **Simple Swaps:** You can use any type of noodle in this dish, such as instant ramen noodles (cooked separately) or even spaghetti, boiled until just a few minutes short of al dente consistency and drained. Or, use leftover rice in place of noodles, for drunken-style fried rice.

# THAI-STYLE STIR-FRIED MACARONI

## Pad Macaroni

PREP TIME: 10 MINUTES · COOK TIME: 15 TO 20 MINUTES

NUT-FREE

I have fond childhood memories of ordering *pad macaroni* at every chance I got while growing up in Bangkok. The ingredients might seem strange at first, but it's essentially just as Thai a dish as the far more well-known Pad Thai. It's basically Thai-Italian fusion, in the same way that Pad Thai is Thai-Chinese fusion: Italian noodles (pasta) cooked in a Thai-style sauce and in a particularly Asian way: stir-fried in a wok. The combination might sound strange, but give it a try—it's delicious and a big hit with kids, probably because it's not very spicy. **SERVES 4**

9 ounces macaroni (Thais use straight, smooth macaroni noodles about 1¼ inches long when dry, about 3 inches long when cooked; see Ingredient Tip 1)

3 tablespoons ketchup

1 to 2 tablespoons Sriracha sauce (see page 17)

1 tablespoon soy sauce

2 teaspoons fish sauce

2 tablespoons vegetable oil

2 garlic cloves, finely minced

1 onion, cut into ¼-inch slices

½ carrot, peeled and cut crosswise into thin slices

9 ounces chicken breast, pork, or shrimp cut into bite-size pieces (see Ingredient Tip 2)

3 scallions, cut into 2-inch lengths, white parts also halved lengthwise, kept separate

1 large egg

2 tomatoes, cored and each cut into 8 wedges

Ground white pepper, for serving

1. Place a large pot of water over high heat to boil for the pasta. When the water reaches a rolling boil, add a pinch of salt and the pasta, and cook the pasta until just about 1 minute short of al dente. Drain well, rinse in cold running water, and set aside.

2. Meanwhile, in a small bowl, mix the ketchup, Sriracha, soy sauce, and fish sauce until well combined. Set aside.

*continued*

3. In a large, flat-bottomed wok or skillet over high heat, heat the oil until shimmering.

4. Add the garlic, and stir-fry until light golden, 30 seconds to 1 minute.

5. Add the onion and carrot, and continue to stir-fry until the vegetables are softened, 2 to 3 minutes.

6. Add the chicken and scallion whites, and continue stir-frying until the meat is just browned and the scallion whites are softened, 3 to 4 minutes.

7. Push all the ingredients to the sides of the wok or skillet with a wooden spoon. Break the egg into the middle of the wok and lightly scramble it (it's okay if there are still some separate bits of white and yolk) for about 30 seconds, and then toss the scrambled egg together with the rest of the ingredients until evenly distributed.

8. Add the cooked pasta and sauce, and toss everything well until the macaroni is evenly coated.

9. Add the tomatoes and scallion greens, and continue stir-frying just until the tomatoes and scallion greens are slightly softened, about 1 minute.

10. Serve immediately, with a sprinkle of white pepper on top.

**Ingredient Tip 1:** *If you can't find the macaroni described above, you can also use bucatini, perciatelli, or bigoli broken into 1- to 2-inch lengths, or a short pasta such as ziti, mostaccioli, or smooth penne. Don't use elbow macaroni (the type used in American mac and cheese), as they are too small and thin.*

**Ingredient Tip 2:** *If using shrimp, quickly stir-fry the shrimp separately just until pink, about 2 minutes, and stir into the noodles just before serving.*

# CHIANG MAI CURRY WITH EGG NOODLES AND CHICKEN

*Khao Soi Gai*

SPICE LEVEL: MILD

PREP TIME: 15 MINUTES · COOK TIME: ABOUT 20 MINUTES

NUT-FREE

This one-dish meal—a rich, mild yellow curry served over springy fresh egg noodles and garnished with some of the same noodles, fried till crisp—originates from the northern Thai town of Chiang Mai. The dish allegedly has Burmese or Muslim origins; the fact that it is usually made with either chicken or beef (not pork) seems to support the latter. It's typically made with fresh, flat egg noodles about ¼ inch wide, but if you can only find thin, round fresh egg noodles, those will work. Typically, it's made with bone-in, skin-on chicken legs and thighs, so feel free to use 2 pounds of those instead, if you prefer, simmering for about 20 to 30 minutes. **SERVES 4**

**FOR THE FRIED-NOODLE GARNISH**

¼ pound fresh egg noodles (preferably flat ones about ¼ inch wide)

Neutral vegetable oil, for frying

**FOR THE CURRY PASTE**

4 dried red long chiles (2 to 3 inches long), stemmed

1 tablespoon coriander seed

2 green cardamom pods, inner seeds only

1 teaspoon cumin seed

1 tablespoon curry powder

3 tablespoons chopped shallot

2 tablespoons chopped fresh ginger

1 tablespoon chopped garlic

1 tablespoon chopped fresh turmeric (from about a 1-inch piece; there's no need to peel it), or 1 teaspoon dried ground turmeric

2 teaspoons cilantro root or stem

Pinch salt

**FOR THE CURRY**

1 (14-ounce) can coconut milk, divided

1 pound boneless chicken (light or dark meat), cut into 1-inch pieces

2 cups water or Basic Thai Chicken Stock (page 91)

2 tablespoons palm sugar, light brown sugar, or granulated sugar

2 tablespoons soy sauce

1 tablespoon fish sauce

1 pound fresh egg noodles (preferably flat ones about ¼-inch wide)

2 scallions, green part only, cut into ¼-inch rings, for serving (optional)

¼ cup roughly chopped fresh cilantro, for serving (optional)

*continued*

**TO MAKE THE FRIED-NOODLE GARNISH**

1. Using your hands, tear the fresh egg noodles in shorter strands, about 5 to 6 inches long.

2. In a wok, heavy-bottomed pot, or Dutch oven over medium-high heat, heat 1 to 2 inches of oil to 375°F (or until a cube of bread browns in the oil in about 30 seconds).

3. Fry the noodles in 2 to 3 batches, turning and flipping with a metal spider or slotted spoon, until evenly crisp and golden-brown, 20 to 30 seconds.

4. Transfer the fried noodles to a paper towel–lined plate to drain, and set aside.

**TO MAKE THE CURRY PASTE**

1. In a small, dry skillet over low heat, toast the chiles, coriander seed, cardamom pods, and cumin seed until fragrant and slightly browned, 1 to 2 minutes. Remove from the heat and let cool.

2. In a mortar and pestle (or spice grinder), grind the toasted chiles and spices to a powder. Transfer to a small bowl, mix in the curry powder, and set aside.

3. In a mortar and pestle (or blender or food processor), grind the shallot, ginger, garlic, turmeric, cilantro root or stem, and salt to form a paste. Mix into the dry spices, and set aside.

**TO MAKE THE CURRY**

1. Scoop about 3 to 4 tablespoons coconut cream from the top of the coconut milk into a medium saucepan (if there's no cream, just use the coconut milk). Add the curry paste, and heat over medium-low heat until fragrant and small simmering pockets of oil separate out, about 3 to 5 minutes.

2. Add the chicken, turn the heat to medium, and toss to brown, 2 to 3 minutes.

3. Add the remaining coconut milk and the water.

4.  Add the sugar, soy sauce, and fish sauce, and adjust the seasoning to taste, as necessary.

5.  Bring to a simmer and cover, simmering until the chicken is cooked through, about 10 minutes.

6.  Meanwhile, bring a large pot of water to a boil and cook the noodles until done, about 2 minutes. Drain the noodles well and divide them among 4 serving bowls.

7.  Top each bowl of noodles with an equal portion of the curry and chicken, sprinkle with the scallions (if using) and cilantro (if using), and serve.

**Serving suggestion:** *Besides the scallions and cilantro, other optional accompaniments are sliced shallots, lime wedges, chopped pickled mustard greens (sold in Asian markets in clear plastic bags and packed in liquid), and an oily fried chili paste (you can buy this in Asian markets, or simply sprinkle some Ground Roasted Chili Powder, page 230, on top).*

**Simple Swaps:** *You can use 2 tablespoons store-bought Khao Soi curry paste in place of homemade, adjusting seasonings as necessary, or 2 tablespoons store-bought Panang Curry Paste or Red Curry Paste, store-bought or homemade (page 130), mixed with 1 tablespoon curry powder. To make it with beef, use 1 pound beef cut into 1-inch chunks and simmer until the beef is cooked through, 20 to 30 minutes.*

**Dial Up the Heat:** *Northern Thai dishes are generally milder, but I use 6 chiles when I make this dish, which ups the spice rating to about 2 chiles. You can also add fried chili paste when serving to increase the heat to taste.*

# CHAPTER FOUR

# Soups and Salads

Unlike in Western cuisines, in Thailand, soups and salads are not a separate course but part of a family-style meal with other dishes, including steamed or sticky rice. The one exception is soups with noodles, which are a one-dish meal, often eaten for a quick lunch at a street-side stand.

Diners often add a bit of rice to their soup or salad, or spoon some soup or salad over their serving of rice. That's why Thai soups and salads are so highly flavored. That doesn't mean that you can't serve them without rice, but you might need to adjust the seasoning accordingly.

Soups are often flavored by infusing them with whole pieces of herbs and aromatics, such as lemongrass, galangal, and kaffir lime leaves. Thais leave these in when serving and know that they're not meant to be eaten. It's up to you whether to leave them or remove them before serving.

Since their flavors are so bold, layered, and complex, you might be surprised to discover how quick and easy these dishes are—all can be made in less than 30 minutes, many in less than 15 minutes!

# Thai Salads

As with soups, Thai salads are not an appetizer or starter course but part of a larger meal, either served with steamed rice or sticky rice. Like the soups, they are highly flavored because they are not intended to be eaten alone.

The term "salad" is applied a bit loosely to Thai cuisine since there are several distinct types of Thai dishes that are all called "salad" when translated to English, but most don't correspond directly to the Western concept of a bowl of raw, leafy greens seasoned with a dressing (the one exception being Salad Khaek, page 116).

The many types of Thai salad include *yum*, *phla*, *lahb*, *nam tok*, and *tum*. Though they're often served with whole leaves of lettuce or cabbage, they generally contain more protein and less greens than a Western salad. Most of them contain no oil in the dressing, so they are light and healthy.

A *yum* can be made with just about anything, cut into bite-size pieces and dressed in a light, tangy dressing of fresh lime juice, fish sauce, sugar, and fresh chiles.

*Lahb* is a specialty from northeastern Thailand's Isaan region, made with minced meat, fresh mint, cilantro, scallions, and the key ingredient, roasted rice powder.

A *nam tok* ("waterfall") salad, meanwhile, is like lahb but made with grilled, thinly sliced meat instead of poached minced meat.

*Phla* is a sort of Thai-style ceviche, in which the fresh lime juice cooks thinly sliced seafood or beef. These days, most cooks par-cook the seafood or beef before adding it to the lime dressing. These salads are usually made with lemongrass.

Finally, *tum* refers to salads that have been pounded, traditionally in a large clay mortar with a wooden pestle. The most well-known example is Som Tum (page 99), the popular Isaan salad most often made with crisp, young green papaya, but this kind of lightly pounded salad can be made with most anything, even a mixture of fresh fruit.

These salads should all be made just before serving, as they're intended to be eaten warm or at room temperature, and most don't keep or reheat well. You can, however, prepare individual components ahead of time and assemble just before serving.

# BASIC THAI CHICKEN STOCK

## Nam Stock Gai

SPICE LEVEL: NONE

PREP TIME: 5 MINUTES · COOK TIME: 1 HOUR

GLUTEN-FREE · SOY-FREE · NUT-FREE

This simple, light stock is unsalted since it is used as the base for highly flavored soups, sauces, and curries. Make a big batch and keep some frozen so you'll have it on hand whenever you need it. It's better to use this stock for Thai cooking than high-sodium canned broths or stocks with seasonings such as bay leaves and thyme, which clash with Thai flavors. In fact, it's better to just use water in Thai cooking, adjusting seasoning in the dish as necessary, if you don't have the time to make this neutral stock. **MAKES ABOUT 2 QUARTS**

2 quarts (8 cups) water

2 pounds bone-in, skin-on chicken pieces (either a mixture of white and dark meat or only dark, for example breasts and legs or legs and thighs)

1 large yellow onion, peeled and diced

2 celery stalks, diced

4 large garlic cloves, peeled and crushed with the flat side of a chef's knife

1. In a large stockpot over medium heat, bring all the ingredients just to a simmer.

2. Turn the heat to low and cook at a very gentle simmer, covered, for at least 1 hour or up to 1½ hours.

3. Strain out all solids using a fine-mesh strainer (reserve the cooked chicken meat for another use).

4. Defat the stock: You can do this either by using a fat separator while the stock is still hot or by refrigerating it for several hours until it's completely chilled. The fat will harden on the surface and can be simply spooned off and discarded.

5. This stock can be refrigerated for up to 4 days or frozen for up to 6 months.

*continued*

**Recipe Tip:** *This is a great way to use up leftover roast chicken or turkey: Just swap in the leftover meat and bones for the raw chicken. The stock will have a different flavor–not quite as fresh or complex–but it still works, particularly when used as the base for highly flavored curries and soups.*

**Leftover Tip:** *Use the cooked chicken meat leftover from making this broth in any curry or fried rice, Pra Ram (page 166), Tom Kha Gai soup (page 95), Chicken and Napa Cabbage Salad with Crispy Shallots (page 106), in a simple Quick Congee Rice Porridge (page 62), or simply eat it with Jasmine Rice (page 53), topped with some Chili, Garlic, and Lime Sauce (page 236).*

# HOT-AND-SOUR TOM YUM
# SOUP WITH SHRIMP

## Tom Yum Goong

SPICE LEVEL: HOT

PREP TIME: 10 MINUTES · COOK TIME: 5 MINUTES

GLUTEN-FREE · SOY-FREE · NUT-FREE

This popular soup, wonderfully tangy and aromatic with lemongrass and fresh cilantro, is surprisingly quick and easy to make. A key ingredient is Nam Prik Pao (Roasted Chili Paste, page 240), which can be found in most Asian markets, sometimes labeled "Roasted Chili Paste in Soybean Oil," "Chili Paste in Oil," or "Chili Jam." Store-bought pastes sometimes come in "mild," "medium," and "hot." By nature it's quite a spicy soup, and it's traditionally made with fresh red chiles floating in it; you can omit those to tone it down a bit, or use less chili paste (2 to 3 tablespoons). **SERVES 4**

4 cups water or Basic Thai Chicken Stock (page 91)

6 (⅛-inch-thick) slices unpeeled fresh galangal, bruised with the butt of a chef's knife (optional)

3 lemongrass stalks (bottom 3 inches only), bruised with the flat side of a chef's knife

2 fresh kaffir lime leaves (optional)

4 tablespoons Roasted Chili Paste (page 240 or store-bought)

4 to 5 tablespoons fish sauce, to taste

1 cup fresh button mushrooms cut into ¼-inch slices, or canned straw mushrooms, drained and halved or left whole

12 large raw shrimp, deveined (peeled or unpeeled, as you prefer; if removing the shell, leave tails on for a nicer presentation)

¼ cup freshly squeezed lime juice (or to taste)

1 or 2 fresh red Thai bird's-eye chiles, stemmed, seeded, and each thinly sliced lengthwise into 4 strips (optional)

¼ cup fresh cilantro leaves, for serving

1. Place the water, galangal (if using), lemongrass, and kaffir lime leaves (if using) in a medium saucepan or Dutch oven. Cover and bring just to a boil over high heat. Turn the heat to low and simmer for 5 minutes.

*continued*

2. Remove and discard the galangal, lemongrass, and lime leaves at this point if you intend to serve the soup without them (Thais leave them in, but they're just for flavoring, not for eating).

3. Stir in the chili paste until it dissolves, and then stir in the fish sauce. Add the mushrooms, and simmer for 1 minute.

4. Add the shrimp, and simmer for 1 minute more.

5. Remove from the heat and stir in the lime juice and chiles (if using). Adjust the seasoning, as needed, with additional fish sauce or lime juice.

6. Serve immediately in small bowls, sprinkling each serving with cilantro.

**Ingredient Tip:** *If you're not a fan of mushrooms, you can omit them altogether. Halved cherry tomatoes are an optional addition.*

**Ingredient Tip:** *If using frozen, precooked shrimp, use Basic Thai Chicken Stock (page 91) instead of water.*

**Recipe Tip:** *You can freeze any extra lemongrass and sliced galangal so that you'll have it on hand for making this soup whenever you feel like it. They can be stored in the freezer, wrapped in plastic wrap and stored in resealable freezer bags, for up to 6 months.*

**Veggie Version:** *To make this soup vegetarian, omit the shrimp and roasted red chili paste (which contains shrimp) and season with salt or soy sauce instead of fish sauce. Or for a vegan chili paste, you can make your own: Follow the recipe for Roasted Chili Paste (Nam Prik Pao, page 240), omitting the dried shrimp, shrimp paste, and fish sauce and seasoning with salt or soy sauce instead. Vegemite or Marmite can be used in place of the shrimp paste.*

# COCONUT-GALANGAL SOUP WITH CHICKEN

### *Tom Kha Gai*

SPICE LEVEL: MILD

PREP TIME: 10 MINUTES · COOK TIME: 10 MINUTES

GLUTEN-FREE · SOY-FREE · NUT-FREE

This creamy, coconut milk–based soup is relatively mild, fragrant with galangal, and tangy with fresh lime juice. Thais leave lemongrass, galangal, and kaffir lime leaves in when serving, but you can remove and discard them before adding the chicken and mushrooms, if you prefer; they're not intended for eating. Optional additions include fresh or canned baby corn or sliced bamboo shoots. SERVES 4

2 cups Basic Thai Chicken Stock (page 91) or water

1½ cups coconut milk

10 (⅛-inch-thick) slices unpeeled fresh galangal, bruised with the butt of a chef's knife

4 kaffir lime leaves, bruised by rolling between your fingers

1 stalk lemongrass (bottom 3 inches only), bruised with the flat side of a chef's knife

3 tablespoons fish sauce

¾ pound boneless, skinless chicken (breast or thigh meat), cut into bite-size pieces (about 2 inches by ½ inch by ⅛ inch)

1 cup quartered fresh button mushrooms (optional)

1 to 2 fresh red Thai bird's-eye chiles, stemmed, seeded, and thinly sliced lengthwise (optional)

2 tablespoons freshly squeezed lime juice

½ cup fresh cilantro leaves

2 scallions, green part only, sliced crosswise into ¼-inch-thick rings (about 2 tablespoons; optional)

1.  In a medium saucepan or Dutch oven over medium heat, bring the stock, coconut milk, galangal, kaffir lime leaves, and lemongrass just to a boil. Turn the heat to low and simmer, covered, for 5 minutes.

2.  Remove and discard the galangal, lime leaves, and lemongrass at this point if you intend to serve the soup without them (Thais leave them in, but they're just for flavoring, not for eating).

*continued*

3. Stir in the fish sauce, chicken, mushrooms (if using), and chiles (if using). Bring back to a simmer over medium heat, and then turn the heat to low and simmer, covered, until the chicken is cooked, about 3 minutes.

4. Remove from the heat and stir in the lime juice. Adjust the seasoning, if necessary, with additional fish sauce and lime juice.

5. Serve immediately in small bowls, sprinkling each serving with cilantro and scallions (if using).

**Recipe Tip:** *If you have leftover chicken meat from making Basic Thai Chicken Stock (page 91), you can just stir in 1½ cups of it in place of the raw chicken.*

**Ingredient Tip:** *You can also use fresh oyster mushrooms or canned straw mushrooms.*

**Ingredient Tip:** *It's better to use water than a canned chicken broth, since Basic Thai Chicken Stock is unsalted and store-bought stocks can contain seasonings that clash with Thai flavors.*

# SIMPLE SOUP WITH TOFU, MEATBALLS, AND VEGETABLES

*Gaeng Jeud Taohu Moo Sup*

SPICE LEVEL: NONE

PREP TIME: 10 MINUTES · COOK TIME: 15 MINUTES

NUT-FREE

This soup might be simple and easy to make, but it's anything but boring. Though the Thai name means "bland soup," it's actually very flavorful–it's just not spicy! This is one of my ultimate comfort foods, and it's a staple in many Thai households. I like to load mine up with soft tofu, pork meatballs, Napa cabbage, daikon radish, and bean thread noodles to make it into a one-dish meal, but many simpler versions exist. You can make it with just tofu and meatballs, tofu and noodles, etc. As part of a meal, it's a nice soup to balance out spicy dishes. **SERVES 4 TO 6**

**FOR THE MEATBALLS**

½ pound ground pork

1 tablespoon finely chopped cilantro root or stem

1 tablespoon finely minced garlic (about 1 large clove)

2 teaspoons soy sauce

2 teaspoons fish sauce

¼ teaspoon ground white pepper

**FOR THE SOUP**

4 cups water or Basic Thai Chicken Stock (page 91)

1 tablespoon thin soy sauce (see page 8)

1 tablespoon fish sauce

1 scallion, white and light green parts very thinly sliced, dark green part cut into ¼-inch-thick slices

2 cups (2-inch) Napa cabbage pieces

1 cup daikon radish, cut into ¼-inch-thick slices (optional)

10 ounces egg tofu or soft silken tofu, broken into 1½-inch chunks

⅓ cup fresh cilantro leaves, for serving (optional)

Fried Garlic in Oil (page 234), for serving (optional)

¼ teaspoon ground white pepper, for serving

**TO MAKE THE MEATBALLS**

In a medium bowl, mix well to combine all the meatball ingredients. Set aside.

*continued*

## TO MAKE THE SOUP

1. In a large stockpot over high heat, bring the water, soy sauce, fish sauce, and the white and light green parts of the scallion to a boil.

2. Turn the heat to low, and drop the meatball mixture by the scant tablespoonful into the soup (no need to roll the meat into round balls; they are typically cooked in loose, irregular shapes). You will have about 12 to 14 meatballs. Simmer gently until meatballs are no longer pink, 2 to 3 minutes.

3. Stir in the cabbage and daikon radish (if using), and simmer, covered, until the vegetables are tender, 8 to 9 minutes (3 to 4 minutes if not using daikon radish).

4. Gently stir in the tofu, and simmer just until heated through, about 1 minute.

5. Serve immediately, garnishing each serving, as desired, with a few cilantro leaves, some of the dark green scallion slices, a little fried garlic and fried garlic oil (if using), and a pinch of ground white pepper.

**Ingredient Tip:** Egg tofu is very soft tofu that is usually sold in clear plastic tubes in Asian markets (often in Japanese or Korean markets). It's usually spooned into the soup in large chunks, using the edge of the spoon to scoop off each piece.

**Variation:** To add bean thread noodles (glass noodles) in addition to (or instead of) the tofu, radish, and cabbage, soak 1 ounce of noodles in warm water for 10 minutes, then add to the soup at the same time as the tofu.

**Veggie Version:** Use only soy sauce and salt to flavor the soup, omit the meatballs, and add bean thread noodles, if desired, as described above.

# GREEN PAPAYA SALAD

## Som Tum

SPICE LEVEL: MILD

PREP TIME: 10 MINUTES

GLUTEN-FREE · SOY-FREE

This popular salad from the northeastern Thai Isaan region is typically served with Grilled Chicken (page 45) or Grilled Pork (page 214) and Sticky Rice (page 55). There are many variations, some with crab or pickled fish, but this simple version is the most widely known. It's often searingly spicy, but this recipe produces a relatively mild salad. Adjust the number and type of chiles to suit your taste (I usually use 4 to 6 chiles). Traditionally it is made using a tall clay mortar and wooden pestle, but it's not required, as it's a rather bulky, single-use item that I don't recommend buying unless you're a Som Tum addict! **SERVES 4**

**FOR THE DRESSING**

2 garlic cloves

2 fresh Thai bird's-eye chiles, stemmed, seeded, and coarsely chopped

1 tablespoon palm sugar or light brown sugar

1 tablespoon small dried shrimp (optional)

3 tablespoons fish sauce (or to taste)

3 tablespoons freshly squeezed lime juice (or to taste)

**FOR THE SALAD**

5 cups grated green papaya (from a 1½-pound papaya)

1 cup grated carrot

20 green beans (4 ounces), trimmed and cut into 1½-inch lengths

8 cherry tomatoes, halved

½ cup roasted peanuts, coarsely chopped

**TO MAKE THE DRESSING**

1. In a granite mortar and pestle, pound the garlic and chiles together lightly (or chop them finely, if you don't have a mortar and pestle). There's no need to turn them into a paste; just crush them slightly.

2. Add the sugar, and mix well.

*continued*

3.  Add the dried shrimp (if using), and pound again until the shrimp fall apart into small pieces (chop the shrimp separately, and then mix them in if you don't have a mortar and pestle).

4.  Mix in the fish sauce and lime juice, adjust the seasoning to taste, and set aside.

**TO MAKE THE SALAD**

1.  In a large wooden or metal salad bowl, slightly pound the papaya and carrot with the bottom of a bottle, rolling pin, or any other large, blunt, slightly heavy object. Your goal is not to pulverize the papaya but just to bruise it slightly, so that it will release its flavor and absorb the dressing better.

2.  Add the green beans and tomatoes, and pound again, gently, to bruise the green beans and tomatoes as well.

3.  Drizzle the dressing over the salad, and toss to distribute it evenly. Sprinkle the peanuts over the salad, and serve immediately.

**Simple Swaps:** If you can't find green papaya, you can use 6 cups grated carrot, or substitute the papaya with green mango, jicama, cabbage, radish, green apples, or any other crisp, firm, neutral-flavored vegetable or fruit.

**Dial Up (or Down) the Heat:** Some Thais use as many as 6 or 7 bird's-eye chiles in a single serving of Som Tum—but that's only for the very brave! Feel free to gradually increase the amount (or omit them entirely) to suit your taste.

**Veggie Version:** For a vegetarian or vegan version, omit the dried shrimp and use salt instead of fish sauce for seasoning.

# BEAN THREAD NOODLE SALAD

*Yum Woon Sen*

SPICE LEVEL: MEDIUM

PREP TIME: 5 MINUTES, PLUS 15 MINUTES TO SOAK · COOK TIME: 5 MINUTES

GLUTEN-FREE · NUT-FREE

This is one of my favorite Thai salads—light, tangy, and refreshing, yet substantial enough to serve as a light meal together with some Jasmine Rice (page 53). For a spicier salad, use 1 teaspoon of the chili powder; for a milder salad, use ¼ teaspoon chili powder or omit it entirely. **SERVES 4**

**FOR THE DRESSING**

2 tablespoons freshly squeezed lime juice, plus more for the salad if needed

4 teaspoons fish sauce, plus more for the salad if needed

½ teaspoon palm sugar or granulated sugar

½ teaspoon Ground Roasted Chili Powder (page 230)

**FOR THE SALAD**

3 ounces bean thread noodles (glass noodles), soaked in warm water for 10 to 15 minutes to soften

¼ pound (4 ounces) ground pork or chicken

¼ cup water

8 medium raw shrimp

¼ cup very thinly sliced shallot

½ cup celery leaves, roughly chopped

½ cup grated carrot (in thin strips about ⅛ inch wide and 3 to 4 inches long)

6 cherry tomatoes, halved

2 tablespoons fresh cilantro leaves, roughly chopped

**TO MAKE THE DRESSING**

In a small bowl, stir to combine all the dressing ingredients until the sugar dissolves. Set aside.

**TO MAKE THE SALAD**

1. Drain the softened noodles, and cut them into 5-inch lengths. Set aside.

*continued*

2. In a small saucepan over medium-high heat, put the pork in the water and bring to a simmer. Simmer gently, using the edge of a wooden spoon or spatula to break up the meat into smaller pieces, until cooked, about 2 minutes. Set aside to cool (do not drain).

3. Bring a large pot of water to a boil over high heat.

4. When the water is boiling, ready a fine-mesh strainer. Place the noodles inside the strainer, and dunk them into the boiling water. As soon as the noodles are softened and translucent, about 1 minute, remove them from the boiling water in the strainer, drain them well, and transfer them to a large bowl.

5. Add the shrimp to the boiling water, turn the heat to low, and cook until pink and opaque, about 2 minutes. Drain the shrimp well, and add them to the bowl with the noodles.

6. Add the shallot and cooked pork (and its liquid) to the bowl with the shrimp and noodles, and toss to wilt the shallot a bit.

7. Add the dressing, celery leaves, carrot, tomatoes, and cilantro, and toss again to combine well. Adjust the seasoning, as needed, with additional lime juice and fish sauce. Serve warm or at room temperature.

**Serving Suggestion:** *Serve with a bit of Fried Garlic (page 234) and Fried Garlic Oil drizzled on top.*

**Recipe Tip:** *A handheld julienne grater, such as a Kiwi Pro Slice (see page 20), works well for grating the carrot.*

# THAI-STYLE SHRIMP CEVICHE

## *Phla Goong*

SPICE LEVEL: MEDIUM

PREP TIME: 10 MINUTES · COOK TIME: 5 MINUTES

GLUTEN-FREE · SOY-FREE · NUT-FREE

Traditionally, this type of salad is made with raw shrimp or other seafood, which gets cooked by the acidic lime juice, much like the *ceviche* of Peruvian cuisine. These days, most cooks blanch the seafood to partially cook it before mixing it with the chili-lime dressing. The smoky depth of Roasted Chili Paste (page 240) is balanced by the brightness of the citrus juice and the lemongrass–if you're a fan of Tom Yum Soup (page 93), you'll love this salad, as the flavors are similar. Using shell-on shrimp gives much more flavorful, tender results, but you can also use peeled shrimp. SERVES 4

### FOR THE DRESSING

4 tablespoons fish sauce

3 tablespoons freshly squeezed lime juice

2 tablespoons Roasted Chili Paste (Nam Prik Pao, page 240, or store-bought)

2 fresh Thai bird's-eye chiles, stemmed, seeded, and finely chopped (optional)

½ teaspoon Ground Roasted Chili Powder (page 230; optional)

### FOR THE SALAD

2 quarts (8 cups) water

1 tablespoon salt

1 pound large, shell-on, fresh or frozen raw shrimp

⅔ cup very thinly sliced lemongrass

1 large shallot, very thinly sliced

½ cup fresh cilantro leaves, roughly chopped

½ cup fresh mint leaves, roughly torn

### TO MAKE THE DRESSING

In a small bowl, stir to combine all the dressing ingredients until the sugar dissolves. Adjust the seasoning to taste, if necessary. Set aside.

### TO MAKE THE SALAD

1.  In a large saucepan over high heat, bring the water and salt to a boil.

*continued*

2.  Add the shrimp and blanch just until barely pink but only partially cooked, about 1 minute if fresh, 2 to 3 minutes if frozen. Drain and set aside until cool enough to handle, and then peel and devein the shrimp (leaving the tails on, if desired).

3.  Toss the shrimp in the dressing while still warm, and let sit for 2 to 3 minutes. Toss with the lemongrass, shallot, cilantro, and mint before serving.

**Simple Swaps:** *You can make this salad with scallops, squid, fish, or thinly sliced beef instead of shrimp.*

# SPICY THAI-STYLE TUNA SALAD

## Yum Tuna

SPICE LEVEL: MILD

PREP TIME: 10 MINUTES

GLUTEN-FREE · SOY-FREE · NUT-FREE

This simple, no-cook salad brings together the convenience of canned tuna and the bold vibrancy of Thai flavors for a quick-yet-delicious salad that can be eaten with rice as part of a larger meal, used as a sandwich filling, or served in lettuce cups as an appetizer or snack. **SERVES 4**

2 (12-ounce) cans solid tuna packed in water, drained and broken into large chunks

6 cherry tomatoes, quartered

½ cup fresh cilantro leaves

½ cup chopped celery leaves (optional)

¼ cup very thinly sliced shallot

1 scallion, very thinly sliced crosswise

½ cup freshly squeezed lime juice

2 tablespoons fish sauce

4 teaspoons very thinly sliced lemongrass (from the bottom 3 inches of 1 stalk)

1 teaspoon Ground Roasted Chili Powder (page 230), or to taste

1. In a medium bowl, toss to combine all the ingredients.

2. Serve immediately or refrigerate for up to 2 days.

# CHICKEN AND NAPA CABBAGE SALAD WITH CRISPY SHALLOTS

*Yum Gai*

SPICE LEVEL: MILD

PREP TIME: 10 MINUTES · COOK TIME: 5 MINUTES

GLUTEN-FREE · SOY-FREE

A refreshing salad, made with shredded chicken, this dish can be served as part of a larger meal or by itself as a light, healthy meal. Poaching cooks the chicken quickly while keeping it juicy and tender. The tender chicken, crisp cabbage, crunchy peanuts, and fried shallots make for an interesting interchange of flavors and textures. This is also a great way to use up leftover chicken (or any other meat) from another recipe, for example Basic Thai Chicken Stock (page 91). **SERVES 4**

**FOR THE DRESSING**

3 tablespoons freshly squeezed lime juice

2 tablespoons fish sauce

1 teaspoon palm sugar or granulated sugar

1 fresh red Thai bird's-eye chile, stemmed, seeded, and finely chopped, or ¼ to 1 teaspoon Ground Roasted Chili Powder (page 230)

**FOR THE SALAD**

1½ cups water

½ teaspoon salt

½ pound boneless, skinless chicken breast fillets

3 cups julienned Napa cabbage

½ cup grated carrot

¼ cup thinly sliced fresh mint leaves

¼ cup roasted peanuts, coarsely chopped or slightly crushed in a mortar and pestle

2 tablespoons fresh cilantro leaves

2 tablespoons thinly sliced scallion (green part only)

Crispy Fried Shallots (page 235 or store-bought), for serving

**TO MAKE THE DRESSING**

In a small bowl, stir to combine all the dressing ingredients until the sugar dissolves. Set aside.

1.  In a small saucepan over high heat, bring the water and salt to a boil.

2.  Add the chicken, turn the heat to low, and gently poach until the chicken is cooked, about 5 minutes. Remove from the heat and set aside to cool.

3.  When the chicken is cool enough to handle, tear it into shreds using your fingers.

4.  In a medium bowl, toss to combine the shredded chicken, dressing, cabbage, carrot, mint, peanuts, cilantro, and scallion, coating everything evenly.

5.  Sprinkle the Crispy Fried Shallots on top, and serve warm or at room temperature.

# POMELO SALAD WITH TOASTED COCONUT AND MINT

*Yum Som Oh*

SPICE LEVEL: MILD

PREP TIME: 5 MINUTES · COOK TIME: 5 MINUTES

GLUTEN-FREE · SOY-FREE

This is an elegant, refreshing salad that looks beautiful when served. A pomelo resembles an oversize grapefruit, about 8 inches in diameter, but it's more fragrant, less juicy, and far less sour; it's sweet enough to be eaten as-is. Like grapefruit, it comes with either pink or yellow flesh; you can use either for this salad, but pink is a bit sweeter and makes for a more attractive presentation. Many variations of this recipe exist, many with dried or fresh shrimp, but I prefer this purer, simpler version that lets pomelo's delicate flavor shine. **SERVES 4**

**FOR THE DRESSING**

4 tablespoons freshly squeezed lime juice

3 tablespoons fish sauce

2 teaspoons palm sugar or light brown sugar

1 teaspoon Ground Roasted Chili Powder (page 230; optional)

**FOR THE SALAD**

¼ cup unsweetened coconut flakes

1 large pomelo or 2 large pink grapefruits, peeled and torn into bite-size pieces (about 5 cups; see Simple Swaps and Ingredient Tip)

1 shallot, thinly sliced

2 tablespoons roasted peanuts, roughly chopped or slightly crushed in a mortar and pestle

½ cup fresh mint leaves, roughly torn if large

**TO MAKE THE DRESSING**

In a small bowl, stir to combine all the dressing ingredients until the sugar dissolves. Set aside.

1.  In a dry skillet over medium-low heat, toast the coconut, shaking the skillet constantly to prevent scorching, until fragrant and lightly browned, about 2 minutes. Remove from the heat, transfer to a small bowl, and let cool.

2.  In a medium bowl, toss to combine the cooled toasted coconut with the dressing, pomelo, shallot, peanuts, and mint leaves. Serve immediately.

**Serving Suggestion:** *Serve on lettuce leaves, sprinkled with Crispy Fried Shallots (page 235 or store-bought).*

**Simple Swaps:** *If you can't find pomelo, you can use grapefruit, but you might need to reduce the amount of lime juice in the dressing, or eliminate it entirely (use the juice released by the grapefruit instead).*

**Ingredient Tip:** *To prepare the pomelo, cut an X-shape into the top and use your fingers or the tip of a knife to peel back the rind. Remove and discard the thick, fluffy white pith. You can then gently peel open each segment and remove the pulp with your fingers, discarding the thick skin surrounding each segment (if using grapefruit, you'll need a knife for this part). The remaining flesh is ready for use in this recipe or eating out-of-hand.*

**Veggie Version:** *For a vegetarian or vegan version, season with salt instead of fish sauce.*

# NORTHEASTERN THAI-STYLE GROUND PORK SALAD

## *Lahb Moo*

SPICE LEVEL: MILD

PREP TIME: 10 MINUTES · COOK TIME: 5 MINUTES

GLUTEN-FREE · SOY-FREE · NUT-FREE

Tangy, refreshing *lahb*, usually served with steamed Sticky Rice (page 55) and an assortment of raw or lightly steamed vegetables, is a favorite from northeastern Thailand's Isaan region. The roasted rice powder is a key ingredient in this recipe for the right smoky, earthy taste and slightly crunchy texture. It's sold in many Asian markets (sometimes labeled as "Toasted Rice Powder"), or you can easily make your own from uncooked jasmine rice or sticky rice (see page 55). The recipe as written makes a mild version; use up to 4 teaspoons chili powder for a spicier salad. SERVES 4

¼ cup water

¾ pound ground pork

3 tablespoons freshly squeezed lime juice

2 tablespoons fish sauce

2 tablespoons Roasted Rice Powder (page 16)

1 teaspoon Ground Roasted Chili Powder (page 230)

½ cup very thinly sliced shallot (about 2 large shallots)

1 scallion, very thinly sliced crosswise

½ cup fresh mint leaves, roughly chopped if large

¼ cup fresh cilantro leaves

1. In a small saucepan over high heat, bring the water to a boil.

2. Add the pork and cook, stirring continuously, until browned, about 2 minutes. Use the edge of a wooden spoon or spatula to break up the pork into smaller pieces as it cooks. Remove from the heat.

3. Stir in the lime juice, fish sauce, rice powder, and chili powder.

4. Stir in the shallot, scallion, mint, and cilantro.

5. Adjust the seasoning to taste, as necessary, by adding more lime juice, fish sauce, or chili powder. Serve warm or at room temperature.

**Ingredient Tip:** *A mandoline makes slicing the shallot quick and easy.*

**Simple Swaps:** *You can use ground chicken, turkey, beef, duck, lamb, or crumbled firm tofu in place of the ground pork.*

**Serving Suggestion:** *Serve with steamed Sticky Rice (page 55) or Jasmine Rice (page 53) and any of the following: green beans, cucumber, or large wedges of raw Napa cabbage. Thais use the cabbage leaves to scoop up the lahb. Another idea: Serve small portions in iceberg lettuce cups as an appetizer or a party finger food.*

# GRILLED EGGPLANT SALAD

## Yum Makhuea Yao

SPICE LEVEL: MILD

PREP TIME: 10 MINUTES · COOK TIME: 10 TO 15 MINUTES, DEPENDING ON METHOD

GLUTEN-FREE · NUT-FREE · SOY-FREE

For this dish, eggplant is grilled until slightly charred and smoky, then served in a tangy chili-lime dressing. Sometimes it's made with ground pork or dried shrimp, but this version uses just eggplant, so it's quite easy to make vegetarian or vegan by simply replacing the fish sauce with salt. In Thailand, it's made with long, green eggplants; this recipe works best with any long Asian eggplant, but you can use globe or Italian eggplants too. It's a great addition to any cookout if you've already got the grill going. Use up to 1 teaspoon chili powder for a spicier salad. **SERVES 4**

### FOR THE DRESSING

3 tablespoons fish sauce

3 tablespoons freshly squeezed lime juice

2 teaspoons palm sugar or light brown sugar

¼ teaspoon Ground Roasted Chili Powder (page 230; optional)

### FOR THE SALAD

2 long Asian (Chinese or Japanese) eggplants, 1 large globe eggplant, or 2 small Italian eggplants

Vegetable oil, for brushing and oiling

½ cup fresh cilantro leaves, roughly chopped

1 large shallot, very thinly sliced

### TO MAKE THE DRESSING

In a small bowl, stir to combine all the dressing ingredients until the sugar dissolves. Set aside.

1. Prepare a charcoal or gas grill, heat a stovetop grill pan over medium-high heat, or preheat the oven to 400°F.

2. If using long Asian eggplant, cut them in half lengthwise. If using globe or Italian eggplant, quarter them lengthwise.

3. Brush the eggplant pieces lightly and evenly with oil.

4. Oil the grill, add the eggplant, and cook, turning occasionally to cook evenly, until slightly charred on the outside and tender enough to pierce easily with the tip of a paring knife, but not mushy, about 10 minutes. (If you don't have a grill or grill pan, cook under a broiler on high for 5 to 10 minutes or roast on a baking sheet at 400°F for about 15 minutes.)

5. When cool enough to handle, cut the eggplant crosswise into 2-inch chunks. Arrange the pieces on a serving platter, scatter the cilantro and shallot around the eggplant pieces, and drizzle the dressing on top. Serve warm or at room temperature.

**Serving Suggestion:** *This salad is traditionally served with hardboiled eggs, quartered lengthwise. It's often also made with small dried shrimp, ground pork, or large poached shrimp; feel free to add them. Some people even make a sort of Thai-style baba ghanoush by scooping the cooked eggplant out of the charred skins and mashing it together with the dressing; that would make a great party dip, perhaps with some crispy shrimp chips or pork crackling. Another optional topping: Sprinkle the final dish with Fried Garlic (page 234).*

**Simple Swaps:** *If you're one of those people who detest cilantro, you can use fresh mint leaves instead (in this and any of the salad recipes in this chapter).*

# GRILLED STEAK SALAD

## *Yum Nuea Yang*

SPICE LEVEL: MEDIUM

PREP TIME: 10 MINUTES · COOK TIME: 5 MINUTES · TOTAL TIME: 20 MINUTES

GLUTEN-FREE · SOY-FREE · NUT-FREE

This salad, with its spicy, tangy chili-lime dressing, is one of my favorite dishes—so quick and easy to make, with such tasty results. It's a great use for any leftover Crying Tiger Grilled Steak (page 205) or any grilled meat leftover from a cookout. Adding 1 tablespoon Roasted Rice Powder (page 16 or store bought) and 2 tablespoons thinly sliced lemongrass turns this into Nuea Nam Tok (Waterfall Beef Salad), the northeastern Thai version of this dish, essentially a *lahb* with grilled instead of minced meat. Use 1 teaspoon chili powder for a spicier salad. **SERVES 4**

### FOR THE DRESSING

3 tablespoons freshly squeezed lime juice

2 tablespoons fish sauce

½ teaspoon Ground Roasted Chili Powder (page 230)

1 teaspoon palm sugar or granulated sugar

### FOR THE SALAD

1 pound thin flank, strip, hanger, or flap steak

4 tablespoons thinly sliced shallot

2 scallions, very thinly sliced

4 tablespoons fresh cilantro leaves, coarsely chopped

1 medium tomato, cut into wedges

4 tablespoons fresh mint leaves, coarsely chopped

### TO MAKE THE DRESSING

In a small bowl, stir to combine all the dressing ingredients until the sugar dissolves. Set aside.

## TO MAKE THE SALAD

1. Prepare a charcoal or gas grill or stovetop grill pan over medium-high heat.

2. Grill the steak to medium-rare (130°F on an instant-read thermometer), about 2 minutes. Remove from the heat and let rest for 3 minutes.

3. Slice the steak across the grain into thin strips (about ¼ inch wide and 2 inches long).

4. In a medium bowl, toss to combine the steak, dressing, shallot, scallions, cilantro, tomato, and mint. Serve warm.

**Serving Suggestion:** *Serve on a bed of lettuce leaves, accompanied by thinly sliced cucumber.*

**Veggie Version:** *Swap the steak for slices of grilled or fried mushrooms, tofu, or tempeh, and replace the fish sauce with salt or soy sauce for a vegan version.*

# MIXED SALAD WITH PEANUT DRESSING

## Salad Khaek

SPICE LEVEL: MILD

PREP TIME: 10 MINUTES · COOK TIME: 5 MINUTES

GLUTEN-FREE · SOY-FREE · VEGETARIAN

This unusual salad from southern Thailand is the exception to the rule that Thai salads are protein-heavy, without a base of leafy greens, and it is simple, refreshing, and delicious. It's traditionally made with thinly sliced fried potatoes, but a good-quality store-bought potato chip or shoestring potato stick does the job. The peanut dressing is essentially a lighter version of Satay Peanut Sauce (page 243), so my shortcut method simply uses that sauce as the base, thinning it with water and brightening it with tangy tamarind and freshly squeezed lime juice. **SERVES 4**

**FOR THE DRESSING**

½ cup Satay Peanut Sauce (page 243 or store-bought)

2 tablespoons water

2 teaspoons tamarind paste (page 26 or store-bought)

1 teaspoon freshly squeezed lime juice

Pinch salt

**FOR THE SALAD**

4 cups sturdy green lettuce (such as iceberg), cut into bite-size pieces

2 hardboiled eggs, quartered

1 (3-inch) piece cucumber, cut into ¼-inch slices (about ½ cup)

½ cup snow peas (optional)

6 cherry tomatoes, halved

1 scallion, green part cut into ¼-inch rings, white part very thinly sliced

¾ cup good-quality potato chips, slightly crumbled into bite-size pieces, or shoestring potato sticks

1.  In a small saucepan over low heat, combine the peanut sauce, water, and tamarind paste. Stir until the sauce has softened and thinned, about 1 minute.

2.  Remove from the heat, and stir in the lime juice and salt. Adjust the seasoning to taste with additional salt, tamarind paste, or lime juice, as necessary. Set aside to cool.

TO MAKE THE SALAD

1.  Place the lettuce in a large salad bowl, and arrange the eggs, cucumber, snow peas (if using), tomatoes, and scallion on top.

2.  Just before serving, sprinkle the potato chips or shoestring potatoes on top, add the dressing, and toss well to coat evenly.

**Variations:** *This salad is often made with crisp Fried Tofu as well, either home-made (page 32) or store-bought. Other optional ingredients include bean sprouts, carrots, and Crispy Fried Shallots (page 235 or store-bought).*

# CHAPTER FIVE

# Curries

What distinguishes many Thai curries from Indian curries, from which they are descended, is their use of coconut milk (whose creamy richness tempers the chiles' heat) and their emphasis on fresh aromatics and herbs rather than dried spices. Some curries, such as panang, choo chee, and prik khing, are thicker and drier and are used for sauces and stir-fries, while yellow and green curries are more liquidy. A third type, common in Thailand though less familiar elsewhere, is lighter, thinner, and more soup-like, made without coconut milk; Jungle Curry (page 138) is an example.

Although it depends on how much paste is used and spice levels vary from brand-to-brand in store-bought pastes, generally yellow and mussamun curry are the mildest, red and panang curries are spicier, and green and jungle curries are the spiciest.

Though satisfying and complex, these curries are surprisingly quick and easy to make; add some Jasmine Rice (page 53), and you can have a satisfying one-dish meal on the table in less than half an hour. In fact, I rarely order curries in a Thai restaurant since they're so simple to make at home. They're also incredibly versatile—though each type of curry is traditionally made with certain protein-and-vegetable combinations, you can use whatever you'd like. Suggestions are given in each recipe.

# Curry Pastes

Thai curry pastes are mostly built from the same base elements: garlic, shallots, lemongrass, and galangal, but it's the proportions—and the remaining ingredients—that give each type its unique color and flavor. Turmeric gives yellow curries their bright hue; red curries get their rich tone and smoky flavor from roasted, dried red chiles; and green curries use fresh green chiles for a brighter, tangier profile.

It's not hard to make the pastes from scratch, and they will add an intensely fresh and aromatic quality to your curries that no store-bought paste can equal. You can make a large batch and refrigerate it in an air-tight glass jar, with plastic wrap pressed against the surface, for up to two weeks or freeze it in plastic freezer bags for up to three months. (Tip: Freeze curry paste in 1-tablespoon portions that will be easy to use without defrosting.) Frozen paste, however, does lose freshness and potency. If you plan to make curry pastes regularly, a granite mortar and pestle (see page 19) is a good—and inexpensive—investment. While more labor-intensive, it fully releases and blends flavors and gives the right consistency (not as smooth as a machine-made paste, but that's okay). The second-best option is a spice grinder and a blender (you'll need both since a blender can't grind dried spices). A small food processor also works, if making larger batches.

But if you're short on time or can't find all the ingredients, there's nothing wrong with using store-bought paste. In fact, it's better to use one than to make your own with a lot of omissions or random substitutions (I've seen curry paste recipes calling for ketchup and other bizarre ingredients—please don't go there!). Look for pastes in plastic tubs or bags, or glass jars, rather than canned pastes, which don't taste very fresh. Mae Ploy is a good brand. Store-bought pastes tend to be saltier and spicier than homemade, so adjust amounts and other seasonings in the following recipes as necessary when using them. If using homemade pastes, use 3 to 4 tablespoons per 4 servings; start out with 1 to 2 tablespoons store-bought paste, adding more, to taste, as necessary.

Besides the basic building block for curries, curry pastes are also great for quick stir-fries, flavorful fried rice, or versatile sauces.

## USING LEMONGRASS

Lemongrass, especially when it isn't particularly fresh, can be tough and woody. When making curry pastes, use only the bottom 3 inches of each stalk, cutting off and discarding the fibrous top and knobby bottom. Then peel off and discard the tougher outer layer of each remaining piece, slice the tender interior in half lengthwise and then again to form 4 thin, long pieces, and slice each of these pieces crosswise to chop it finely. If using frozen lemongrass, use it directly, without defrosting, as it gets a bit wet and soggy when defrosted and can make pounding your paste more difficult. Some Asian markets sell ground or sliced lemongrass in plastic bags in either the frozen or refrigerated section—very convenient if you are making curry paste!

## CHOOSE YOUR SPICE LEVEL

While some curries (such as yellow, mussamun, and panang) are inherently less spicy than others (including green, red, and water-based curries), you can adjust the spice level on any of these curries by using more (up to about ¼ cup) or less (as little as 1 teaspoon) curry paste. If you make your own curry pastes, you can control the spice level there as well by using fewer chiles or less spicy varieties. Don't omit chiles entirely from a paste or curry, however, or it will no longer truly be a curry. If, on the other hand, any curry turns out not hot enough for your tastes, you can add fresh red chiles, stemmed, seeded, and thinly sliced lengthwise, during the last few minutes of simmering, or serve the curry together with Spicy Fish Sauce (page 233) and Pickled Chiles in Vinegar (page 231).

## CHOOSE YOUR PROTEIN

Though suggestions for traditional pairings are given in each curry recipe, you can swap in whatever proteins and vegetables you prefer. When using any meat, cut the meat into thin slices, against the grain (except for mussamun curry, which usually is made with cubes of stew meat and cooked for a bit longer). When using chicken, dark meat will remain more tender and juicy during cooking but might require a slightly longer cook time than white meat. If using fish, cut into large chunks and add to the curry only during the last few minutes of cooking. Shrimp should be peeled and deveined before use and added during the last 2 minutes of cooking. For vegetarian and vegan curries, choose firm tofu, tempeh, or seitan, cut into 1-inch cubes, or cubes of fluffy fried tofu, sold in Asian markets in the refrigerated section. You can also make curries with no protein at all, and just an abundance of mixed vegetables.

For making your own curry pastes, a few tips to keep in mind:

Recipe Tip: If using a blender rather than a mortar and pestle, you might need to add a little bit of water—about 1 tablespoon—to facilitate grinding.

Ingredient Tip: Use a Microplane grater to zest kaffir limes, avoiding the inner white pith.

# BASIC RED GAENG KUA CURRY PASTE

## Nam Prik Gaeng Kua

PREP TIME: 15 MINUTES, PLUS 15 MINUTES TO SOAK

GLUTEN-FREE · SOY-FREE · NUT-FREE

This could be considered the "mother" curry paste from which the others evolved. It contains no dried spices, only dried red chiles, fresh aromatics, and shrimp paste. It is a basic ingredient in many other curry pastes, curries, and stir-fries. Without dried spices, such as coriander and cumin, it pairs much better with seafood than curry pastes that do contain them; those tend to work better with meat. MAKES ABOUT ½ CUP

8 to 10 dried red chiles (2 to 3 inches long), stemmed and seeded

1 teaspoon salt

2 tablespoons finely chopped lemongrass (from the bottom 3 inches of 2 stalks)

4 teaspoons finely chopped galangal

1 tablespoon cilantro root or stem

1 teaspoon kaffir lime zest

½ cup thinly sliced shallot (about 2 large shallots)

¼ cup thinly sliced garlic (about 4 large cloves)

1 teaspoon shrimp paste (optional, but recommended)

1. In a small bowl, soak the chiles in hot water until softened, 10 to 15 minutes.

2. Squeeze the soaked chiles well to remove excess water. In a mortar and pestle or spice grinder, pulverize them together with the salt.

3. In the mortar and pestle or a blender, pound or blend the chiles with the lemongrass, galangal, cilantro root or stem, and kaffir lime zest to form a paste.

4. Add the shallots, garlic, and shrimp paste (if using), and pound or blend again. The final paste should be relatively smooth, with no large chunks or fibers (but a paste made in a mortar will not be as smooth as a machine-made paste).

# JUNGLE CURRY PASTE

*Nam Prik Gaeng Pa*

PREP TIME: 15 MINUTES, PLUS 15 MINUTES TO SOAK

NUT-FREE

This paste is used to make the lighter, thinner Jungle Curry (page 138), which is particularly spicy, since it contains no coconut milk. This version uses both dried and fresh chiles. You can adjust the number and type of dried chile (New Mexico, California, and Anaheim dried chiles are milder, Thai dried chiles are hotter) to tone down the fire. Or, you can simply use less paste when you make the curry. MAKES ABOUT ¼ CUP

10 dried red chiles (2 to 3 inches long), stemmed and seeded

4 to 6 fresh green Thai bird's-eye chiles or 1 to 2 large green jalapeños or serranos, stemmed and chopped

1 teaspoon salt

2 tablespoons finely chopped lemongrass (from the bottom 3 inches of 4 stalks)

1 tablespoon finely chopped galangal

1 tablespoon finely chopped fingerroot (grachai; see page 15)

¼ cup thinly sliced shallot (from 1 large shallot)

2 tablespoons thinly sliced garlic (about 2 large cloves)

1 teaspoon shrimp paste (optional)

1. In a small bowl, soak the dried chiles in hot water until softened, 10 to 15 minutes.

2. Squeeze the soaked chiles well to remove excess water. In a mortar and pestle or blender, pulverize the soaked chiles together with the fresh green chiles and the salt.

3. Add the lemongrass, galangal, and fingerroot, and pound or blend to form a paste.

4. Add the shallot, garlic, and shrimp paste (if using), and pound or blend again. The final paste should be relatively smooth, with no large chunks or fibers (but a paste made in a mortar will not be as smooth as a machine-made paste).

# CHOO CHEE CURRY PASTE

*Nam Prik Choo Chee*

PREP TIME: 15 MINUTES, PLUS 15 MINUTES TO SOAK

GLUTEN-FREE · SOY-FREE · NUT-FREE

This paste is essentially Basic Red Gaeng Kua Curry Paste (page 122) with the addition of ground white peppercorn and toasted dried coconut. It is used to make Choo Chee Curry (page 140), a thick, creamy curry redolent of coconut, which is usually served over seafood. **MAKES ABOUT ¼ CUP**

2 dried red chiles (2 to 3 inches long), stemmed and seeded

½ teaspoon salt

4 tablespoons toasted coconut flakes (see Note)

1 teaspoon white peppercorns

4½ teaspoons finely chopped lemongrass (from the bottom 3 inches of 2 stalks)

2 teaspoons finely chopped galangal

½ teaspoon kaffir lime zest

½ teaspoon cilantro root or stem

¼ cup thinly sliced shallot (from 1 large shallot)

2 tablespoons thinly sliced garlic (about 2 large cloves)

½ teaspoon shrimp paste (optional, but recommended)

1. In a small bowl, soak the chiles in hot water until softened, 10 to 15 minutes.

2. Squeeze the soaked chiles well to remove excess water. In a mortar and pestle or spice grinder, pulverize the chiles together with the salt.

3. Add the toasted coconut flakes and white peppercorns, and pound or grind until even.

4. In the mortar and pestle or a blender, pound or blend the chile-coconut mixture with the lemongrass, galangal, kaffir lime zest, and cilantro root or stem to form a paste.

5. Add the shallot, garlic, and shrimp paste (if using), and pound or blend again. The final paste should be relatively smooth, with no large chunks or fibers (but a paste made in a mortar will not be as smooth as a machine-made paste).

**Note:** *Toasted coconut flakes are sold in health food stores, Asian markets, or online. They are larger pieces, not the same as shredded or grated coconut. That said, if you can only find untoasted coconut flakes or shredded or grated dried coconut, you can toast them yourself in a dry skillet over medium-low heat until they are a rich golden brown, about 2 minutes, shaking the skillet frequently to prevent burning. Make sure, in any case, that they are unsweetened and unseasoned.*

**Recipe Shortcut:** *If you have some Basic Red Gaeng Kua Curry Paste (page 122 or store-bought) on hand, you can just grind the white peppercorn and toasted coconut flakes in a mortar and pestle or spice grinder, and then mix the resulting powder into ¼ cup of the Basic Red curry paste.*

# PRIK KHING CURRY PASTE

### *Nam Prik Pad Prik Khing*

PREP TIME: 10 MINUTES, PLUS 15 MINUTES TO SOAK

GLUTEN-FREE · SOY-FREE · NUT-FREE

This red curry paste is less spicy than the standard Red Curry Paste (page 130). It is often used in stir-fries, such as Spicy Prik Khing Stir-Fried Green Beans (page 162), and usually fried in oil instead of coconut milk, for a drier sauce. Although the name means "ginger stir-fry," the paste itself is never made with ginger, and prik khing stir-fries don't usually contain ginger either; the origin of the name is unclear. This paste can be substituted in any recipe with a smaller amount (to compensate for the difference in spice level) of Red Curry Paste (page 130). **MAKES ABOUT ¼ CUP**

4 dried red chiles (2 to 3 inches long), stemmed and seeded

1 teaspoon salt

1 teaspoon white peppercorns

1 tablespoon finely chopped lemongrass (from the bottom 3 inches of 2 stalks)

1 tablespoon finely chopped galangal

2 teaspoons kaffir lime zest (from 2 or 3 kaffir limes)

½ cup thinly sliced shallot (about 2 large shallots)

¼ cup thinly sliced garlic (about 4 large cloves)

2 teaspoons shrimp paste (optional)

1. In a small bowl, soak the dried chiles in hot water until softened, 10 to 15 minutes.

2. Squeeze the soaked chiles well to remove excess water. In a mortar and pestle or spice grinder, pulverize them together with the salt.

3. Add the peppercorns, and pound or grind to form an even paste.

4. In the mortar and pestle or a blender, pound or blend the chile mixture with the lemongrass, galangal, and kaffir lime zest to form a paste.

5. Add the shallot, garlic, and shrimp paste (if using), and pound or blend again. The final paste should be relatively smooth, with no large chunks or fibers (but a paste made in a mortar will not be as smooth as a machine-made paste).

# YELLOW CURRY PASTE

### Nam Prik Gaeng Garee

PREP TIME: 15 MINUTES, PLUS 15 MINUTES TO SOAK · COOK TIME: 5 MINUTES

GLUTEN-FREE · SOY-FREE · NUT-FREE

This mild curry paste is of Indian origin. "Garee" is the Thai version of the word "curry," referring to the yellow curry powder that it contains. The turmeric adds to the yellow color and warm flavor. If you can find fresh turmeric, it will give much better results than ground. The pungent shrimp paste can be omitted, but it really adds depth and pulls the other flavors together. **MAKES ABOUT ¼ CUP**

7 dried red chiles (2 to 3 inches long), stemmed and seeded

1 tablespoon coriander seed

2 teaspoons cumin seed

1 teaspoon fennel seed

1 teaspoon salt

½ teaspoon white peppercorns

1 tablespoon finely chopped lemongrass (from the bottom 3 inches of 2 stalks)

1 tablespoon finely chopped galangal

1 tablespoon finely chopped fresh turmeric, or 1 teaspoon ground turmeric

⅓ cup thinly sliced garlic (about 8 to 10 cloves)

3 tablespoons thinly sliced shallot (about 1 large shallot)

½ teaspoon shrimp paste (optional, but recommended)

1 tablespoon yellow curry powder

1. In a small bowl, soak the chiles in hot water until softened, 10 to 15 minutes.

2. Meanwhile, in a small, dry skillet over low heat, toast the coriander, cumin, and fennel until fragrant, 2 to 3 minutes. Remove from the heat and let cool completely.

3. Squeeze the chiles well to remove excess water. In a mortar and pestle or spice grinder, pulverize them together with the salt.

4. Add the toasted coriander, cumin, and fennel and the peppercorns to the chile-salt mixture, and pound or grind to form an even powder.

5. In the mortar and pestle or a blender, pound or blend the chile mixture with the lemongrass, galangal, and turmeric to form a smooth paste.

6. Add the garlic, shallot, and shrimp paste (if using), pound or blend again, and then thoroughly mix in the curry powder. The final paste should be relatively smooth, with no large chunks or fibers (but a paste made in a mortar will not be as smooth as a machine-made paste).

# RED CURRY PASTE

*Nam Prik Gaeng Pehd*

PREP TIME: 15 MINUTES, PLUS 15 MINUTES TO SOAK · COOK TIME: 5 MINUTES

GLUTEN-FREE · SOY-FREE · NUT-FREE

The Thai name of this paste means "spicy curry paste," and it is indeed one of the fieriest. There are actually many different types of red curry paste in Thai cooking, but this is one of the most widely used and versatile; it's an ingredient in many other recipes, including Satay Peanut Sauce (page 243) and Fish Cakes (page 41). **MAKES ABOUT ¼ CUP**

10 dried red chiles (2 to 3 inches long), stemmed and seeded

1 tablespoon coriander seed

1 teaspoon cumin seed

6 dried Thai bird's-eye chiles or dried cayenne or piri piri peppers

1 teaspoon salt

1 teaspoon white peppercorns

2 tablespoons finely chopped lemongrass (from the bottom 3 inches of 4 stalks)

1 tablespoon finely chopped galangal

2 teaspoons kaffir lime zest (from 2 or 3 kaffir limes)

1 tablespoon finely chopped cilantro root or stem

½ cup thinly sliced shallot (about 2 large shallots)

¼ cup thinly sliced garlic (about 4 large cloves)

1 teaspoon shrimp paste (optional)

1. In a small bowl, soak the red chiles in hot water until softened, 10 to 15 minutes.

2. Meanwhile, in a small, dry skillet over low heat, toast the coriander and cumin until fragrant, about 2 minutes. Remove from the heat and let cool completely.

3. Squeeze the soaked chiles well to remove excess water. In a mortar and pestle or spice grinder, pulverize the soaked chiles together with the bird's-eye chiles and salt.

4. Add the toasted coriander and cumin and the peppercorns to the chile-salt mixture, and pound or grind to form an even paste.

5. In the mortar and pestle or a blender, pound or blend the chile mixture with the lemongrass, galangal, kaffir lime zest, and cilantro root or stem to form a paste.

6. Add the shallot, garlic, and shrimp paste (if using), and pound or blend again. The final paste should be relatively smooth, with no large chunks or fibers (but a paste made in a mortar will not be as smooth as a machine-made paste).

**Dial Up (or Down) the Heat:** *The long peppers give this paste its vibrant red color, while the short ones give it heat. For a milder paste, you can reduce the number of short chiles or simply omit them.*

# GREEN CURRY PASTE

## Nam Prik Gaeng Kiew Wan

PREP TIME: 15 MINUTES · COOK TIME: 5 MINUTES

GLUTEN-FREE · SOY-FREE · NUT-FREE

This curry paste, made with fresh green chiles, is bright, pungent, and tangy. It's generally one of the spiciest, though you can make it much milder by using green jalapeños or serranos in place of the bird's-eye chiles or just using a smaller amount of the paste when making curry. If you're only going to make one homemade curry paste, this one is really worth the effort, since its fresh, vibrant flavors are mostly lost in store-bought versions. **MAKES ABOUT ½ CUP**

1 tablespoon coriander seed

½ teaspoon cumin seed

1 teaspoon white peppercorns

1 teaspoon salt

2 tablespoons finely chopped lemongrass (from the bottom 3 inches of 2 stalks)

2 tablespoons finely chopped galangal

4 fresh green Thai long chiles (2 to 3 inches long) or 2 green jalapeños, stemmed, seeded, and chopped

8 fresh green Thai bird's-eye chiles (1 inch long) or 3 green serranos, stemmed, seeded, and chopped

2 tablespoons finely chopped cilantro root or stem

1 teaspoon kaffir lime zest (from 2 kaffir limes)

¼ cup thinly sliced garlic (about 6 or 7 cloves)

¼ cup thinly sliced shallot (about 1 or 2 large shallots)

1 teaspoon shrimp paste (optional)

1. In a small, dry skillet over low heat, toast the coriander and cumin until fragrant, about 2 minutes. Remove from the heat and let cool completely.

2. In a mortar and pestle or spice grinder, grind the toasted coriander and cumin together with the peppercorns and salt.

3. If using a mortar and pestle, add the lemongrass and galangal and then pound; add the long and bird's-eye chiles, cilantro root or stem, and kaffir lime zest, and pound again; and finally, add the garlic, shallot, and shrimp paste (if using), and pound once more.

4. If using a blender, add the lemongrass, galangal, long and bird's-eye chiles, cilantro root or stem, kaffir lime zest, garlic, shallot, and shrimp paste (if using), and blend to form a paste. The final paste should be relatively smooth, with no large chunks or fibers.

**Recipe Tip:** *Since this is wetter than curry pastes made with dried chiles, you might not need to add any water if using a blender; however, you can add a bit, in 1-teaspoon increments, to facilitate blending if needed.*

**Dial Up (or Down) the Heat:** *For a spice level closer to what you'd find in Thailand, you can increase the amount of bird's-eye chiles and leave the seeds in both types of chile. For a milder paste, use only green jalapeños (3 to 4 large peppers).*

# PANANG PEANUT CURRY PASTE

## Nam Prik Gaeng Panang

PREP TIME: 15 MINUTES, PLUS 15 MINUTES TO SOAK · COOK TIME: 5 MINUTES

GLUTEN-FREE · SOY-FREE

This curry paste is similar to Red Curry Paste (page 130), but it's milder and sweeter, and it contains crushed peanuts. Sometimes warm spices such as nutmeg or cinnamon are also added. Originally it was used to baste whole chickens as they cooked on an open grill, but today it's chiefly used to make thick curries, usually with thin strips of beef. The peanuts and spices hint at an Indian or Middle Eastern influence. Though the name resembles that of the Malaysian island of Penang, there is no connection.

**MAKES ABOUT ½ CUP**

10 dried red chiles (2 to 3 inches long), stemmed and seeded

1 tablespoon coriander seed

1 teaspoon cumin seed

1 teaspoon salt

1 teaspoon white peppercorns

4 tablespoons ground, unsalted roasted peanuts or smooth, unsalted natural peanut butter

2 tablespoons finely chopped lemongrass (from the bottom 3 inches of 4 stalks)

1 tablespoon finely chopped galangal

1 teaspoon kaffir lime zest (from 2 kaffir limes)

1 teaspoon finely chopped cilantro root or stem

¼ cup thinly sliced shallot (from 1 large shallot)

3 tablespoons thinly sliced garlic (about 4 or 5 cloves)

1 teaspoon shrimp paste (optional)

1. In a small bowl, soak the dried chiles in hot water until softened, 10 to 15 minutes.

2. Meanwhile, in a small, dry skillet over low heat, toast the coriander and cumin until fragrant, about 2 minutes. Remove from the heat and let cool completely.

3. Squeeze the soaked chiles well to remove excess water. In a mortar and pestle or spice grinder, pulverize them together with the salt.

4.  Add the toasted coriander and cumin and the peppercorns to the chile-salt mixture, and pound or grind to form an even paste.

5.  Add the peanuts, and pound or grind until well incorporated.

6.  In the mortar and pestle or a blender, pound or blend the chile mixture with the lemongrass, galangal, kaffir lime zest, and cilantro root or stem to form a paste.

7.  Add the shallot, garlic, and shrimp paste (if using), and pound or blend again. The final paste should be relatively smooth, with no large chunks or fibers (but a paste made in a mortar will not be as smooth as a machine-made paste).

**Recipe Shortcut:** *Mix the ground roast peanuts or peanut butter into ½ cup store-bought or homemade Red Curry Paste (page 130) or store-bought panang curry paste. Store-bought panang pastes usually omit the peanuts.*

**Dial Up (or Down) the Heat:** *Use more or fewer chiles to adjust the spice level.*

**Ingredient Tip:** *If you can only find salted roasted peanuts or salted natural peanut butter, reduce the amount of salt used in the curry paste, but don't omit it entirely since it helps to grind the chiles.*

# MUSSAMUN CURRY PASTE

## Nam Prik Gaeng Mussamun

PREP TIME: 15 MINUTES · COOK TIME: 15 MINUTES

GLUTEN-FREE · SOY-FREE · NUT-FREE

While its exact origins are debated, allegedly the name "mussamun" is related to a variant of the word "Muslim," and this mild, complex curry, which uses spices not found in most Thai dishes, likely has Middle Eastern roots. Unlike most other Thai curry pastes, it contains many dried spices, and all the ingredients, including the fresh aromatics, are roasted for a rich, warm flavor. **MAKES ABOUT ⅓ CUP**

5 to 7 dried red chiles (2 to 3 inches long), stemmed and seeded

1 tablespoon coriander seed

2 teaspoons cumin seed

1 teaspoon white peppercorns

3 green cardamom pods

4 cloves

1 teaspoon salt

½ teaspoon ground cinnamon

½ teaspoon freshly grated nutmeg (use a Microplane grater)

¾ cup thinly sliced shallot (about 4 large shallots)

⅓ cup thinly sliced garlic (about 8 to 10 cloves)

2 tablespoons finely chopped lemongrass (from the bottom 3 inches of 2 stalks)

1 tablespoon finely chopped galangal

1 teaspoon shrimp paste (optional)

1.  In a small dry skillet over medium-low heat, toast the chiles, coriander, cumin, peppercorns, cardamom, and cloves until fragrant, 3 to 4 minutes. Remove from the heat and let cool completely.

2.  When cool, in a mortar and pestle or spice grinder, add the salt to the toasted dried spices and grind to reduce to an even powder.

3.  Mix the cinnamon and nutmeg into the ground spice mixture.

4.  In a dry, nonstick skillet over medium-low heat, roast the shallot, garlic, lemongrass, and galangal, stirring frequently with a wooden spatula, until softened and browned, about 10 minutes. You can add 1 teaspoon water, if necessary, to prevent the aromatics from sticking to the pan.

5. Add the shrimp paste (if using), and continue cooking and stirring until evenly mixed and fragrant, about 1 minute.

6. In a mortar and pestle or blender, blend the ground dried spices with the browned aromatics to reduce to a paste. The final paste should be relatively smooth, with no large chunks or fibers (but a paste made in a mortar will not be as smooth as a machine-made paste).

# JUNGLE CURRY WITH GROUND BEEF AND KABOCHA SQUASH

## Gaeng Pa Nuea Sup Fuk Thong

SPICE LEVEL: MEDIUM

PREP TIME: 10 MINUTES · COOK TIME: 15 MINUTES

GLUTEN-FREE · SOY-FREE · NUT-FREE

This light, fragrant, water-based curry is relatively spicy, without coconut milk's richness to tame the heat. For a milder curry, use less curry paste; for a more Thai-style spice level, use up to 4 tablespoons paste. Originally made with freshwater fish or game meat such as wild boar, today jungle curries are often made with seafood, but this version uses ground meat, kabocha squash, and an assortment of vegetables. Jungle curries are flavored with an abundance of fresh herbs, spices, and aromatics, including Thai holy basil, green peppercorns still on the stalk, and thinly sliced grachai (fingerroot; see page 15). **SERVES 4 TO 6**

2 tablespoons vegetable oil

2 tablespoons homemade Jungle Curry Paste (page 123) or store-bought red curry paste

¾ pound ground beef

4 cups water

2 tablespoons fish sauce (or to taste)

1 tablespoon palm sugar or light brown sugar (or to taste)

2 cups 1-inch chunks peel-on kabocha squash, peeled pumpkin, or any other winter squash

3 tablespoons thinly sliced fingerroot (grachai; optional, but recommended)

1 cup fresh or canned baby corn or sliced bamboo shoots, drained and rinsed (optional)

1 cup green beans in 3-inch lengths

4 (4- to 5-inch-long) branches young green peppercorns (optional, but highly recommended)

2 or 3 fresh kaffir lime leaves, roughly torn (optional)

½ cup roughly torn fresh Thai holy basil leaves or Thai sweet basil leaves

Jasmine Rice (page 53) or Coconut Rice (page 58), for serving

1. In a large saucepan or Dutch oven over medium heat, heat the oil.

2. Add the curry paste and cook, stirring with a wooden spoon, until fragrant, about 30 seconds.

3. Add the ground beef. Cook, using a wooden spoon to break it up into smaller pieces, until browned, about 2 minutes.

4. Add the water, fish sauce, and palm sugar, and bring to a boil.

5. Add the kabocha squash and fingerroot (if using), lower the heat to medium-low, and simmer for 5 minutes.

6. Add the baby corn (if using), green beans, green peppercorns (if using), and kaffir lime leaves (if using), and simmer until the squash and beans are tender, about 5 minutes longer.

7. Turn off the heat, stir in the basil leaves, and serve with Jasmine Rice.

**Simple Swaps:** *Any protein, particularly large chunks of fish, works well in this curry. Other vegetables you could add include eggplant, snow peas, hearts of palm, daikon radish, turnip, bell peppers, broccoli, and cherry tomatoes. You can also add 1 to 2 tablespoons Roasted Rice Powder (see page 16) for a toasty, nutty flavor and slightly thicker consistency.*

**Ingredient Tip:** *Fresh young green peppercorns, still on the stalk, are sold in the refrigerated section of many Asian grocery stores. If you can't find it fresh, it's sometimes available in glass jars as well, packed in brine and labeled as "Pickled Young Green Pepper." Just rinse it and use it in the same way. The peppercorns (but not the stalks) are edible. I think their fragrant spiciness and pleasant crunch really make this dish, so they are worth seeking out.*

# SALMON FILLETS AND SNOW PEAS IN CHOO CHEE CURRY

*Choo Chee Pla Salmon*

SPICE LEVEL: MEDIUM

PREP TIME: 5 MINUTES · COOK TIME: 15 MINUTES

GLUTEN-FREE · SOY-FREE · NUT-FREE

Choo Chee curry sauce is made with undiluted coconut milk, so it's thicker and creamier than other curries and is often served on top of seafood. Toasted coconut in the curry paste gives it a fragrant, nutty flavor (see Note). Here, whole salmon fillets are gently braised directly in the curry for an elegant, one-pan meal that's ready in less than 15 minutes. Feel free to use any type of seafood or thinly sliced, quick-cooking vegetable, adjusting the cooking time as necessary. **SERVES 4**

1 (13.5-ounce) can coconut milk, divided

2 tablespoons Choo Chee Curry Paste (page 124 or store-bought; see Note)

1 tablespoon unrefined coconut oil (preferable) or vegetable oil, if needed (optional)

1 tablespoon palm sugar or light brown sugar

2 teaspoons fish sauce

4 boneless, skinless salmon fillets (5 to 6 ounces each)

1 cup snow peas

2 (4- to 5-inch-long) branches young green peppercorns (see page 18; optional)

2 tablespoons very thinly sliced (chiffonade; see Ingredient Tip) kaffir lime leaves, for serving (optional)

¼ cup fresh Thai sweet or Italian basil, for serving (optional)

Jasmine Rice (page 53), for serving

1. In a large sauté pan (or large, deep skillet with a lid) over medium heat, stir 3 tablespoons of the coconut milk (use the coconut cream that has risen to the top of the milk, if present) with the curry paste just until combined. The pan should be big enough to hold all 4 fillets in a single layer.

2. Simmer, scraping the mixture occasionally with a wooden spoon to prevent it from sticking to the bottom, until fragrant and the coconut milk "cracks" (see page 23), and little pockets of colored oil start to bubble in the coconut

milk, 3 to 5 minutes. If the coconut milk won't "crack," it's okay; move on to step 3. (Optional: You can add 1 tablespoon unrefined coconut oil [preferable] or vegetable oil, and then cook for 1 minute longer, to fake the cracking before moving on to step 3.)

3. Add the remaining coconut milk and the palm sugar and fish sauce, stirring gently to combine thoroughly without disturbing the oil floating on top (if present). Adjust the seasoning as necessary to taste.

4. Add the fish in a single layer, turn the heat to low, and simmer, covered, for 5 minutes. The liquid should come at least halfway up the sides of each fillet; if necessary, you can add up to ½ cup water.

5. Gently flip the fillets over, scatter the peas and green peppercorns (if using) around the fillets, and cook, covered, until the peas are crisp-tender and the fish is cooked through, 3 to 4 minutes longer.

6. Place each fillet in a shallow bowl, and ladle the curry sauce and peas on top. Sprinkle each serving with a little of the sliced kaffir lime leaves (if using) and basil leaves (if using), and serve with Jasmine Rice.

**Note:** *If using store-bought Choo Chee curry paste, you'll need to add about 1 teaspoon ground toasted dried coconut per tablespoon of curry paste if the paste does not contain it. See the Note in the Choo Chee Curry Paste recipe (page 125).*

**Ingredient Tip:** *To chiffonade the kaffir lime leaves (if using), stack 2 on top of each other, roll them up tightly, and slice as thinly as possible.*

**Recipe Shortcut:** *You can also cook the curry sauce (with or without vegetables in it) separately and serve it over grilled, fried, baked, or poached seafood. It's a great way to liven up leftover grilled fish from a cookout!*

# RED CURRY WITH SHRIMP AND PINEAPPLE

## *Gaeng Kua Goong*

SPICE LEVEL: MEDIUM

PREP TIME: 10 MINUTES · COOK TIME: 5 MINUTES

GLUTEN-FREE · SOY-FREE · NUT-FREE

This curry uses Basic Red Gaeng Kua Curry Paste (page 122), a paste that's more suited for seafood since it doesn't contain spices such as coriander and cumin, which Thais generally use in meat-based curries. However, if you don't have the time to make the paste and can't find premade Gaeng Kua paste in stores, you can substitute Red Curry Paste (page 130 or store-bought), using slightly less as it is spicier.

**SERVES 4**

1 to 3 tablespoons Basic Red Gaeng Kua Curry Paste (page 122 or store-bought), or Red Curry Paste (page 130 or store-bought)

2 cups coconut milk, divided

1 to 2 tablespoons unrefined coconut oil (preferable) or vegetable oil, if needed (optional)

1 tablespoon fish sauce

2 teaspoons palm sugar or light brown sugar

½ pound raw shrimp, peeled and deveined

1 cup 1-inch chunks fresh pineapple

¼ cup roughly torn fresh Thai or Italian sweet basil (optional)

Jasmine Rice (page 53), for serving

1. In a medium saucepan or Dutch oven over medium heat, stir the curry paste and 3 tablespoons of the coconut milk (use the coconut cream that has risen to the top of the milk, if present) just until combined.

2. Simmer, scraping the mixture occasionally with a wooden spoon to prevent it from sticking to the bottom, until fragrant and the coconut milk "cracks" (see page 23) and little pockets of colored oil start to bubble in the coconut milk, 3 to 5 minutes. If the coconut milk won't "crack," that's okay; move on to step 3. (Optional: You can add 1 to 2 tablespoons unrefined coconut oil [preferable] or vegetable oil, and then cook for 1 minute longer, to fake the cracking before moving on to step 3.)

3. Add the remaining coconut milk and the fish sauce and palm sugar, stirring gently to combine thoroughly without disturbing the droplets of oil floating on top (if present).

4. Gently stir in the shrimp and pineapple, and simmer just until the shrimp turns pink and opaque and the pineapple is heated through, about 2 minutes. Stir in the basil (if using) at the end of cooking, just before turning off the heat.

5. Adjust the seasoning, as necessary, and serve over Jasmine Rice.

# YELLOW CURRY WITH CHICKEN AND POTATOES

## Gaeng Garee Gai

SPICE LEVEL: MILD

PREP TIME: 10 MINUTES · COOK TIME: 20 MINUTES

GLUTEN-FREE · SOY-FREE · NUT-FREE

This mild, rich, creamy curry is a favorite with Thai kids and is a great "starter" curry for those just getting acquainted with Thai-style curries. It's usually made with potatoes, onions, and bone-in, skin-on dark-meat chicken, which gives a fuller flavor, but for convenience, this recipe calls for boneless, skinless chicken breast. I use 3 to 4 tablespoons paste when I make this, since I like it a bit spicier. **SERVES 4**

2 tablespoons Yellow Curry Paste (page 128 or store-bought)

2 cups coconut milk, divided

1 to 2 tablespoons unrefined coconut oil (preferable) or vegetable oil, if needed (optional)

1 tablespoon fish sauce

1½ teaspoons palm sugar or light brown sugar

1 pound boneless, skinless chicken breast, sliced against the grain into 2-inch chunks

1 large waxy potato, peeled and cut into 1-inch chunks (about 1¾ cups)

1 small yellow onion (or ½ large onion), cut into ¼-inch slices (about ¾ cup)

1 cup water or Basic Thai Chicken Stock (page 91)

2 to 3 teaspoons tamarind paste (page 26 or store bought) or freshly squeezed lime juice if needed

Jasmine Rice (page 53), for serving

1.  In a medium saucepan or Dutch oven over medium heat, stir the curry paste and 3 tablespoons of the coconut milk (use the coconut cream that has risen to the top of the milk, if present) just until combined.

2.  Simmer, scraping the mixture occasionally with a wooden spoon to prevent it from sticking to the bottom, until fragrant and the coconut milk "cracks" (see page 23) and little pockets of colored oil start to bubble in the coconut milk, 3 to 5 minutes. If the coconut milk won't "crack," it's okay; move on to step 3.

(Optional: You can add 1 to 2 tablespoons unrefined coconut oil [preferable] or vegetable oil, and then cook for 1 minute longer, to fake the cracking before moving on to step 3.)

3. Add the remaining coconut milk and the fish sauce and palm sugar, stirring gently to combine thoroughly without disturbing the droplets of oil floating on top (if present).

4. Gently stir in the chicken, and simmer just until the chicken is no longer pink, about 5 minutes.

5. Add the potato, onion, and water or stock. Stir gently to combine, cover, and let simmer until the potato and onion are tender and the chicken is cooked through, 8 to 10 minutes.

6. Adjust the seasoning to taste with fish sauce, sugar, and tamarind paste, as necessary, and serve over Jasmine Rice.

**Serving Suggestion:** *This curry is traditionally served over Steamed Jasmine Rice (page 53), and accompanied by tangy Ajaat (Cucumber Relish, page 242), which helps balance the richness. Sometimes the curry is also sprinkled with Crispy Fried Shallots (page 235).*

**Simple Swaps:** *You can use any protein you prefer in this recipe: beef, lamb, duck, tofu, tempeh, or seafood, for example. If using seafood, add it toward the end of cooking, rather than at the beginning. Vegetables that would work well in this curry include tomatoes, carrots, pumpkin, sweet potato, and broccoli.*

**Ingredient Tip:** *Turmeric (fresh or ground) can stain your hands and nails yellow; wear disposable rubber gloves when handling to prevent that.*

# GREEN CURRY WITH PORK, BAMBOO SHOOTS, AND EGGPLANT

*Gaeng Kiew Wan Moo*

SPICE LEVEL: MEDIUM

PREP TIME: 10 MINUTES · COOK TIME: 20 MINUTES

GLUTEN-FREE · SOY-FREE · NUT-FREE

Piquant and tangy, this curry benefits greatly from using a homemade paste (page 132) rather than store-bought. It's spicier than yellow curries, mussamun, and some red curries. It's usually made with pork, chicken, or fish balls and two different types of Thai eggplant: golf ball–size white ones and tiny, slightly bitter ones that resemble green peas. Since those are difficult to find, this recipe substitutes peas and narrow Asian eggplant (but you can use any kind). The curry's color will be more khaki than bright green. Some recipes add cilantro, basil, or spinach to enhance the color, but I find they throw off the flavor. **SERVES 4**

2 tablespoons Green Curry Paste (page 132 or store-bought)

2 cups coconut milk, divided

1 to 2 tablespoons unrefined coconut oil (preferable) or vegetable oil, if needed (optional)

1 tablespoon fish sauce

½ pound boneless pork, sliced against the grain into ½-inch by 2-inch strips

1 long Asian eggplant, cut into 1-inch cubes (about 1½ cups)

½ cup thin-sliced or julienned strips canned bamboo shoots, rinsed and drained

½ cup fresh or frozen green peas

2 or 3 kaffir lime leaves, roughly torn (optional)

1 cup water or Basic Thai Chicken Stock (page 91)

½ cup fresh Thai sweet basil or Italian basil leaves, roughly torn, plus more for serving (optional)

Palm sugar or granulated sugar, if needed

Jasmine Rice (page 53), for serving

1. In a medium saucepan or Dutch oven over medium heat, stir the curry paste and 3 tablespoons of the coconut milk (use the coconut cream that has risen to the top of the milk, if present) just until combined.

2. Simmer, scraping the mixture occasionally with a wooden spoon to prevent it from sticking to the bottom, until fragrant and the coconut milk "cracks" (see page 23) and little pockets of colored oil start to bubble in the coconut milk, 3 to 5 minutes. If the coconut milk won't "crack," it's okay; move on to step 3. (Optional: You can add 1 to 2 tablespoons unrefined coconut oil [preferable] or vegetable oil, and then cook for 1 minute longer, to fake the cracking before moving on to step 3.)

3. Add the remaining coconut milk and the fish sauce, stirring gently to combine thoroughly without disturbing the droplets of oil floating on top (if present).

4. Gently stir in the pork, and simmer just until the meat is no longer pink, 4 to 5 minutes.

5. Add the eggplant, bamboo, peas, kaffir lime leaves (if using), and water. Stir gently to combine, cover, and let simmer until the eggplant and peas are tender and the pork is cooked through, 8 to 10 minutes. Add the basil leaves (if using) at the end of cooking, just before turning off the heat.

6. Adjust the seasoning to taste with fish sauce, as necessary, and serve over Jasmine Rice. If it seems too spicy, adding a bit of palm sugar or granulated sugar can help balance out the heat.

*continued*

**Serving Suggestion:** *Serve with Jasmine Rice (page 53) and topped with additional fresh Thai (or Italian) basil leaves, if desired. This curry is also lovely served over boiled somen noodles or thin rice vermicelli noodles.*

**Simple Swaps:** *You can use any protein or vegetables you prefer in this recipe. It pairs particularly well with chicken (traditionally it's made with bone-in, skin-on dark meat chicken), shrimp, mussels, and fish or fish balls. Vegetables that would work well in this curry include baby corn, hearts of palm, broccoli, zucchini, green beans, asparagus, snap peas, bell peppers, and yellow summer squash.*

**Dial Up the Heat:** *For extra Thai-style heat, use 3 to 4 tablespoons curry paste and add 1 to 2 fresh Thai long green chiles (2 to 3 inches long), stemmed, seeded, and thinly sliced lengthwise, at the same time as the eggplant, peas, and bamboo.*

**Ingredient Tip:** *The kaffir lime leaves are used just for flavoring and are not intended for eating. You can remove them before serving, if you prefer.*

# RED CURRY WITH ROAST DUCK AND PINEAPPLE

*Gaeng Pehd Bped Yang*

SPICE LEVEL: MEDIUM

PREP TIME: 5 MINUTES · COOK TIME: 10 MINUTES

NUT-FREE

This is a delightful curry that is very quick and easy to make if you have access to a Chinese rotisserie or market that sells roast duck. The sweet, tangy pineapple balances the richness of the duck and the heat of the curry paste. Red curry is one of the most versatile, though, so you can substitute pretty much any meat, seafood, or vegetable protein that you like. It works particularly well with beef and seafood.

**SERVES 4**

2 tablespoons Red Curry Paste (page 130 or store-bought)

2 cups coconut milk, divided

1 to 2 tablespoons unrefined coconut oil (preferable) or vegetable oil, if needed (optional)

1 tablespoon fish sauce

2 teaspoons palm sugar or light brown sugar

1 pound roast duck, cut into ½-inch slices (from ½ Chinese roast duck)

1½ cups fresh pineapple chunks

1½ cups cherry tomatoes

1 cup water or Basic Thai Chicken Stock (page 91)

½ cup fresh Thai or Italian sweet basil (optional)

Jasmine Rice (page 53), for serving

1. In a medium saucepan or Dutch oven over medium heat, stir the curry paste and 3 tablespoons of the coconut milk (use the coconut cream that has risen to the top of the milk, if present) just until combined.

2. Simmer, scraping the mixture occasionally with a wooden spoon to prevent it from sticking to the bottom, until fragrant and the coconut milk "cracks" (see page 23) and little pockets of colored oil start to bubble in the coconut milk, 3 to 5 minutes. If the coconut milk won't "crack," it's okay; move on to step 3.

*continued*

(Optional: You can add 1 to 2 tablespoons unrefined coconut oil [preferable] or vegetable oil, and then cook for 1 minute longer, to fake the cracking before moving on to step 3.)

3. Add the remaining coconut milk and the fish sauce and palm sugar, stirring gently to combine thoroughly without disturbing the droplets of oil floating on top (if present).

4. Gently stir in the duck, pineapple, tomatoes, and water; cover; and simmer just until heated through and the tomatoes start to break down, 6 to 7 minutes. Stir in the basil (if using) at the end of cooking, just after turning off the heat.

5. Adjust the seasoning to taste with fish sauce and sugar, as necessary, and serve over Jasmine Rice.

**Simple Swaps:** *You can use canned pineapple, in a pinch, though fresh is much better in this recipe. Sometimes fresh lychee or rambutan fruit (with the peels and seeds removed) or even grapes are used instead of pineapple, for a sweet and exotic twist. You can use any leftover cooked meat in place of the duck, for example, leftover roast Thanksgiving turkey. Vegetables that work well in red curry include pumpkin or any winter squash, bell peppers, sweet potatoes, and carrots.*

# PANANG PEANUT CURRY WITH BEEF

### Gaeng Panang Nuea

SPICE LEVEL: MILD

PREP TIME: 10 MINUTES · COOK TIME: 10 MINUTES

GLUTEN-FREE · SOY-FREE

This mild curry is thicker and creamier than most other Thai curries, as it is made only with coconut milk and not thinned with any water or broth. The roasted peanuts in the paste give it a warm, nutty flavor. It is one of the few Thai curries that is almost always made with beef, typically in thin strips, and traditionally it does not contain any vegetables. It's so quick and easy to make, but elegant and impressive. If you use a store-bought paste, you'll likely need to add the peanuts yourself since commercial pastes omit the peanuts (see Note). **SERVES 4**

2 tablespoons Panang Curry Paste (page 134, or store-bought panang curry paste, or red curry paste mixed with 1 tablespoon ground roasted peanuts or natural peanut butter; see Note)

1 (13.5-ounce) can coconut milk, divided

1 tablespoon unrefined coconut oil (preferable) or vegetable oil, if needed (optional)

1 tablespoon fish sauce

1 teaspoon palm sugar or light brown sugar

1 pound boneless beef (such as flank steak), sliced against the grain into thin strips (about ½ inch wide and 3 to 4 inches long)

2 (4- to 5-inch-long) branches young green peppercorns (see page 18; optional)

3 to 4 very thinly sliced (chiffonade; see Ingredient Tip) fresh kaffir lime leaves, for serving (optional, but recommended)

1 to 2 red Thai bird's-eye chiles, stemmed, seeded, and sliced lengthwise into thin strips, for serving (optional)

Jasmine Rice (page 53), for serving

3 tablespoons chopped roasted peanuts, for serving (optional)

1. In a medium saucepan or Dutch oven over medium heat, stir the curry paste and 2 tablespoons of the coconut milk (use the coconut cream that has risen to the top of the milk, if present) just until combined.

*continued*

2.  Simmer, scraping the mixture occasionally with a wooden spoon to prevent it from sticking to the bottom, until fragrant and the coconut milk "cracks" (see page 23) and little pockets of colored oil start to bubble in the coconut milk, 3 to 5 minutes. If the coconut milk won't "crack," it's okay; move on to step 3. (Optional: You can add 1 tablespoon unrefined coconut oil [preferable] or vegetable oil, and then cook for 1 minute longer, to fake the cracking before moving on to step 3.)

3.  Gently stir in the remaining coconut milk and the fish sauce and sugar without disturbing the oil on top (if present), return to a simmer, and adjust the seasoning to taste, as necessary.

4.  Add the beef and green peppercorns (if using), stir a few times with a wooden spoon, turn the heat to low, cover, and simmer gently until the beef is just cooked through, about 4 minutes. Be careful not to overcook or the beef can get dry and tough.

5.  Serve sprinkled with the chiffonade of kaffir lime leaves (if using) and the slices of red chile (if using), accompanied by Jasmine Rice. You can also sprinkle each serving with a bit of chopped roasted peanuts, if desired, to enhance the peanut flavor.

**Note:** If using store-bought panang curry paste or red curry paste, you'll need to mix 1 to 2 tablespoons (depending on amount of curry paste used) of ground roasted, unsalted peanuts or smooth, unsalted natural peanut butter into the 2 tablespoons curry paste before using it. If you increase or decrease the amount of curry paste used, the ratio of peanuts to store-bought paste is 1½ teaspoons ground peanuts or peanut butter per tablespoon of curry paste.

**Recipe Tip:** If you want to add something besides meat, whole cherry tomatoes, snow peas, fresh or canned baby corn or bamboo shoots, 1-inch chunks of pineapple, or any other quick-cooking vegetable are good additions. Add them to the pot at the same time as the beef.

**Ingredient Tip:** To chiffonade the kaffir lime leaves (if using), stack them top of each other, roll them up tightly, and slice as thinly as possible.

**Serving Suggestion:** Serve garnished with fried or fresh basil leaves.

# MUSSAMUN CURRY WITH BEEF, SWEET POTATOES, AND PEANUTS

## Gaeng Mussamun Nuea

SPICE LEVEL: MILD

PREP TIME: 10 MINUTES · COOK TIME: 20 MINUTES

GLUTEN-FREE · SOY-FREE

This fragrant, complex curry, made with a paste containing roasted aromatics and warm spices like cinnamon and cardamom, most likely has Middle Eastern or Indian influences ("Mussamun" is allegedly related to the word "Muslim"). Since it's relatively mild, it's popular with Thai children and was my little brother's favorite when we lived in Bangkok. Normally it's a long-cooked dish, but this is a speedy weeknight version that uses a more tender cut of beef so that it doesn't need to be simmered for hours.

**SERVES 4 TO 6**

3 tablespoons Mussamun Curry Paste (page 136 or store-bought)

2 cups coconut milk, divided

1 to 2 tablespoons unrefined coconut oil (preferable) or vegetable oil, if needed (optional)

1 tablespoon fish sauce

2 tablespoons palm sugar or light brown sugar

1 pound lean boneless steak (don't use stew beef), cut into 1-inch cubes

½ pound sweet potato, peeled and cut into ¼-inch-thick slices (about 2 cups)

1 small yellow onion, cut into ¼-inch slices (about 1 cup)

¼ cup water (or as needed to cover)

2 tablespoons tamarind paste (see page 26 or store-bought)

¼ cup roasted peanuts

Jasmine Rice (page 53), for serving

1. In a medium saucepan or Dutch oven over medium heat, stir the curry paste and 3 tablespoons of the coconut milk (use the coconut cream that has risen to the top of the can, if present) just until combined.

2. Simmer, scraping the mixture occasionally with a wooden spoon to prevent it from sticking to the bottom, until fragrant and the coconut milk "cracks" (see page 23) and little pockets of colored oil start to bubble in the coconut milk, 3 to 5 minutes. You can add a little more coconut cream or milk if it gets too dry. If the coconut milk won't "crack," it's okay; move on to step 3. (Optional: You can

add 1 to 2 tablespoons unrefined coconut oil [preferable] or vegetable oil, and then cook for 1 minute longer, to fake the cracking before moving on to step 3.)

3.  Add the remaining coconut milk and the fish sauce and palm sugar, stirring gently to combine thoroughly without disturbing the droplets of oil floating on top (if present).

4.  Gently stir in the beef, sweet potato, onion, and water; cover; and simmer gently over low heat just until the beef is cooked through and the potatoes are tender, about 15 minutes.

5.  Stir in the tamarind paste and peanuts. Adjust the seasoning to taste with fish sauce, sugar, or additional tamarind paste, as necessary, and serve over Jasmine Rice.

**Simple Swaps:** *Traditionally this curry is made with beef, dark-meat (bone-in, skin-on) chicken, or lamb, but it is also good with duck or goat. You could also use meatballs made of ground beef or lamb, for an even quicker-cooking version. The vegetables are usually just onions and either sweet potatoes or waxy potatoes, but feel free to experiment with other starchy root vegetables or winter squash. For a vegetarian version, try 1-inch cubes of tempeh or cubes of fried tofu; omit the fish sauce and season with salt instead.*

**Recipe Tip:** *Some people stir in a bit of fresh pineapple juice at the end of cooking to balance the flavor with a bit of sweetness and acidity. Use only fresh pineapple juice, not bottled or canned.*

**Serving Suggestions:** *You can serve this with Jasmine Rice (page 53) or with roti flatbread. With its warm spices and the beef, this is a rare Thai dish that would pair well with a red wine. Consider a fruity, low-tannin red, such as a Shiraz, Beaujolais, or perhaps a Lambrusco.*

# CHAPTER SIX
# Vegetables and Tofu

Thais eat a wide variety of vegetables, sometimes raw or lightly steamed and dipped in flavorful sauces, such as Chiang Mai's Nam Prik Ong (page 39), or on the side of dishes such as Lahb (page 110). Often, however, they're cooked into dishes that also contain meat or seafood, rather than as a separate, vegetable-only side. And, as usual, these dishes are served with steamed rice and other dishes as part of a family-style meal. Because they are generally mild, they can be used to balance spicier dishes, such as a curry.

In Thai cooking, as in other Asian cuisines, tofu is not thought of as a vegetarian meat substitute (though it also plays that role) but a much-appreciated protein in itself that's often paired with meat or seafood in popular dishes.

The best thing about the dishes in this chapter, most of them stir-fried, is that none take more than 20 minutes to make!

# Vegetarian and Vegan Thai Cooking

Although Thais eat lots of vegetables and many go strictly vegetarian for certain Buddhist festivals, it's more difficult than you might expect to find traditional Thai recipes that are naturally vegetarian or vegan since fish sauce, oyster sauce, and shrimp paste make an appearance as flavor boosters in many otherwise meat-free preparations.

That said, it is not difficult to make minor adjustments so that nearly any Thai dish can be vegetarian or vegan. Vegan fish sauce is available online and in Asian markets, made with mushrooms or seaweed, but you can also simply omit it. In general, it's better to season with salt rather than replace fish sauce with soy sauce in a recipe, unless the recipe already calls for soy sauce as well, or the dish is so highly flavored and colored that the difference in taste and color will not be noticeable.

Many Thai stir-fry dishes call for oyster sauce, replaceable by vegetarian oyster sauces (made from mushrooms) widely available in Asian markets and online, and sometimes labeled as "Vegetarian Stir-Fry Sauce."

As for pungent fermented shrimp paste (*gapi*), it is difficult to substitute, but some have successfully used Vegemite or Marmite as a vegan stand-in. The smell and taste are completely different, but they have a similar consistency and concentrated *umami*-boosting power, so there's a certain logic to the idea.

Apart from those three ingredients, it's incredibly simple to sub tofu, seitan, tempeh, or any other meat-free protein into any curry, soup, salad, or stir-fry. Larger Asian markets offer an incredible variety of soy products in many different textures and flavors.

# STIR-FRIED NAPA CABBAGE

### Pad Galumplee

SPICE LEVEL: NONE

PREP TIME: 5 MINUTES · COOK TIME: 5 MINUTES

NUT-FREE

This was a regular on my mom's roster: a super quick-and-easy vegetable dish that can be whipped up in mere minutes as part of just about any Asian meal. It might sound plain, but it's really flavorful, especially when cooked in a well-seasoned wok, and the sauce it produces is wonderful on steamed rice. Napa cabbage, available in Asian grocery stores and many larger supermarkets, is a more delicate type of cabbage that cooks quickly. SERVES 4

1 head Napa cabbage

3 tablespoons vegetable oil

4 garlic cloves, finely minced

1 tablespoon fish sauce

1 tablespoon soy sauce

1. Cut the cabbage crosswise into narrow strips (about 1½ inches wide and 3 to 4 inches long).

2. In a wok or large skillet over medium heat, heat the oil. Add the garlic, and stir-fry until light golden, about 30 seconds.

3. Add the cabbage, and stir-fry until crisp-tender, 3 to 4 minutes.

4. Add the fish sauce and soy sauce, stir-fry for about 1 minute more, and serve.

**Variations:** Any leafy green will work in this stir-fry, for example bok choy, Chinese broccoli, broccoli rabe, pea sprouts, Swiss chard, kale, spinach, etc. Just adjust the cooking time as necessary for hardier greens.

# STIR-FRIED MIXED VEGETABLES

## Pad Pak Ruam Mit

SPICE LEVEL: NONE

PREP TIME: 10 MINUTES · COOK TIME: 10 MINUTES

NUT-FREE

You can use whatever vegetables you'd like in this dish, but a mixture of different colors and textures gives the best results. To make it vegetarian or vegan, use vegetarian oyster sauce (made with mushrooms, sometimes labeled as "Vegetarian Stir-Fry Sauce") or use only soy sauce. You can find fresh or frozen baby corn in Asian grocery stores—it is worlds better than canned baby corn, so if you can find it, give it a try! If not, canned also works. **SERVES 4**

2 tablespoons vegetable oil

½ onion, cut in ½-inch slices

10 pieces baby corn, halved lengthwise if large

1 cup broccoli florets, cut into 3-inch pieces

½ carrot, peeled and thinly sliced crosswise into thin coins (about ½ cup)

2 cups Napa cabbage, cut into 3-inch pieces

1 cup snow peas

2 tablespoons oyster sauce

2 tablespoons water

1 tablespoon soy sauce

1 teaspoon sesame oil

Jasmine Rice (page 53), for serving

1.  In a large wok or skillet over medium heat, heat the vegetable oil. Add the onion, and stir-fry until softened, about 2 minutes.

2.  Add the baby corn, broccoli, and carrot, and continue stir-frying for another 3 minutes, stirring constantly with a wooden spoon or spatula.

3.  Add the cabbage and snow peas, and stir-fry for 1 minute more.

4.  Add the oyster sauce, water, soy sauce, and sesame oil, and continue stir-frying until all the vegetables are crisp-tender and evenly covered in the sauce, 2 to 4 minutes more.

5.  Serve with Jasmine Rice.

# STIR-FRIED TOFU WITH BEAN SPROUTS

## Taohu Pad Tua Ngoc

SPICE LEVEL: MILD

PREP TIME: 5 MINUTES · COOK TIME: 5 MINUTES

NUT-FREE

This is another quick and easy yet supremely satisfying stir-fry, with soft tofu pieces that soak up the savory sauce and crisp bean sprouts for contrast. To make this dish vegetarian or vegan, use vegetarian oyster sauce or fermented soybean sauce (see page 15). **SERVES 4**

2 tablespoons vegetable oil

4 garlic cloves, minced

15 fried tofu cubes (see Note), halved diagonally to form triangular pieces

2 cups bean sprouts

4 scallions, cut into 2-inch lengths, white parts also halved lengthwise, kept separate

2 or 3 fresh red Thai chiles, serranos, or jalapeños, stemmed and sliced lengthwise into thin strips (optional)

1 tablespoon oyster sauce

1 tablespoon soy sauce

Ground white pepper, for serving (optional)

Jasmine Rice (page 53), for serving

1. In a large wok or skillet over medium heat, heat the oil. Add the garlic, and stir-fry until light golden, 30 to 40 seconds.

2. Add the tofu, bean sprouts, scallion whites, and chiles (if using), and stir-fry until the sprouts are crisp-tender, about 2 minutes.

3. Add the oyster sauce, soy sauce, and dark green scallion parts, and stir-fry just until all the ingredients are mixed and heated through and the scallion greens are slightly softened, 30 seconds to 1 minute.

4. Sprinkle with the white pepper (if using), and serve with Jasmine Rice.

**Note:** *Fried pieces of tofu (usually about 1½ inches to 2 inches square) are sold in Asian markets in the refrigerated section, with all the other types of tofu. If you can't find them, follow the recipe for Fried Tofu on page 32.*

# SPICY PRIK KHING STIR-FRIED GREEN BEANS

## Pad Prik Khing Tua Khaek

SPICE LEVEL: HOT

PREP TIME: 5 MINUTES · COOK TIME: 5 MINUTES

NUT-FREE

*Prik khing* is a type of curry paste that is usually used in stir-fries rather than in coconut milk–based curry soups. Although the word "*khing*" in the name means "ginger," neither the paste nor the stir-fry usually contains ginger—I haven't yet gotten to the bottom of why, though I have heard several different theories. Whatever the story, it's a quick-and-easy route to an intensely flavorful dish. The kaffir lime leaf garnish is optional, but its bright flavor really brings the dish to life. **SERVES 4**

1 pound green beans, trimmed

3 tablespoons vegetable oil

3 tablespoons Prik Khing Curry Paste (page 126 or store-bought; use 2 tablespoons, or less, for a milder dish)

1 tablespoon fish sauce or soy sauce

1 tablespoon palm sugar or granulated sugar

¼ cup water or Basic Thai Chicken Stock (page 91)

3 very thinly sliced (chiffonade; see Note) fresh kaffir lime leaves (optional)

Jasmine Rice (page 53), for serving

1. Cut the beans into 2-inch lengths and set aside.

2. In a large wok or sauté pan over medium heat, heat the oil. Add the curry paste, and stir-fry in the oil, mixing with a wooden spoon, until fragrant, about 2 minutes.

3. Add the green beans, and stir-fry until crisp-tender, about 3 minutes.

4.  Add the fish sauce, sugar, and water, and simmer for another 2 minutes.

5.  Sprinkle with the chiffonade of kaffir lime leaves (if using), and serve with Jasmine Rice.

**Note:** *To chiffonade the kaffir lime leaves, stack them on top of each other, roll them up tightly, and then slice them as thinly as possible.*

**Variations:** *You can add any protein to this dish, cut into bite-size pieces, to make it a one-dish meal. Suggestions include crispy pork belly, tofu, shrimp, chicken, or pork.*

**Simple Swaps:** *If you can't find Prik Khing curry paste, you can use 2 tablespoons Red Curry Paste. It's spicier and contains dried spices that Prik Khing paste does not, but it will work.*

# CHINESE BROCCOLI WITH CRISPY PORK BELLY

## Pad Pak Kha Na Moo Grop

SPICE LEVEL: MILD

PREP TIME: 5 MINUTES · COOK TIME: 5 MINUTES

NUT-FREE

This is one of my all-time favorite dishes: savory chunks of pork belly (*moo grop*, also known as *moo sam chun* or "three-layer pork") with a crisp top layer contrast delightfully with crunchy, slightly bitter Chinese broccoli (*pak kha na*). The easiest way to make this dish is to buy cooked crispy pork belly from a Chinese rotisserie or barbecue joint and have them chop it for you into 1-inch chunks. **SERVES 4**

¾ pound (12 ounces) crispy pork belly (store-bought; see headnote)

3 tablespoons vegetable oil

2 garlic cloves, minced (1 tablespoon)

2 or 3 fresh red Thai chiles, jalapeños, or serranos, stemmed and sliced lengthwise

1 pound Chinese broccoli (gai lan) leaves, cut into 3-inch pieces and stems thinly sliced

2 tablespoons oyster sauce

1 tablespoon soy sauce

1 teaspoon sugar

¼ teaspoon ground white pepper

1. If the pork belly isn't already cut, slice it into 1-inch chunks, each with three layers: the crispy skin on top, lighter meat layer in the middle, and then the darker, leaner meat on the bottom.

2. In a large wok or skillet over medium heat, heat the oil. Add the garlic, and stir-fry until golden brown, about 30 seconds.

3. Add the pork belly and chiles, raise the heat to high, and stir-fry for 30 seconds.

4. Add the Chinese broccoli, and stir-fry until the greens are crisp-tender, 2 to 3 minutes.

5. Add the oyster sauce, soy sauce, and sugar, and stir-fry for 1 minute longer.

6. Sprinkle with the white pepper, and serve immediately.

**Ingredient Tip:** *If you can't find Chinese broccoli, also known as gai lan, you can use broccoli rabe, broccolini, or broccoli.*

**Dial Down the Heat:** *This dish isn't particularly spicy, but you can seed the chiles (or omit them) to make it milder.*

# PRA RAM TOFU AND SPINACH IN PEANUT SAUCE

## Pra Ram Long Song Taohu

SPICE LEVEL: MILD

PREP TIME: 5 MINUTES · COOK TIME: 15 MINUTES

GLUTEN-FREE · VEGAN

The name of this dish means "Bathing" or "Swimming" Rama, referring to green vegetables taking a quick dip in water as they're blanched. Lord Rama, a Hindu deity, is often depicted with green skin. This recipe, rather than blanching, uses a short-cut borrowed from Italian cooking in which the greens are briefly cooked in just a tiny amount of water. Though peanut sauce is very popular in the United States, in Thailand peanut-based sauces are mainly used for dipping Chicken Satay Skewers (page 45), as a dressing for Salad Khaek (page 116), and in this dish. **SERVES 4**

1 (14-ounce) block extra-firm tofu, drained

Fine sea salt

2 tablespoons vegetable oil

2 cups Satay Peanut Sauce (page 243 or store-bought)

¼ cup water, plus an additional ¼ cup if needed

¾ pound mature spinach

Toasted sesame seeds, for serving (optional)

1. Cut the block of tofu in half lengthwise (so you have two thinner blocks), and cut each half into pieces that are approximately 1½ inches by 2 inches.

2. Line a baking sheet with 4 layers of paper towels, and arrange the tofu blocks in a single layer on top of the paper towels. Lightly sprinkle the tofu with salt. Cover with 4 more layers of paper towels and press gently but firmly all over to extract as much water as possible.

3. In a large, nonstick skillet over medium heat, heat the oil. Add the tofu cubes and cook, turning to brown evenly, until crisp and golden on all sides, about 8 minutes. Transfer the tofu to a paper towel–lined plate to drain, and sprinkle lightly with salt.

4. In a small saucepan over low heat, warm the peanut sauce and water, stir-ring together, until thinned and heated through, about 2 minutes. You can add

another ¼ cup additional water, if necessary, to thin the sauce to a pourable consistency. Set aside and cover to keep warm.

5. Rinse the spinach thoroughly under cold running water, and then transfer it to a large wok, sauté pan, or stockpot, with just the water that's still clinging to the leaves. Cook over medium heat, stirring frequently with a wooden spoon, just until the spinach is wilted and bright green, 2 to 3 minutes.

6. Remove from the heat and drain well in a fine-mesh strainer, pressing down on the spinach with a wooden spoon to squeeze out as much water as possible.

7. Divide the spinach among 4 plates, arrange the tofu pieces on top of the spinach, and spoon the warm peanut sauce on top. Sprinkle each serving with sesame seeds (if using) and serve.

**Ingredient Tip 1:** *To make the Satay Peanut Sauce vegan, season with salt or soy sauce instead of fish sauce.*

**Ingredient Tip 2:** *Look for large, dark, mature spinach leaves; they hold up better during cooking than baby spinach, which tends to turn slimy.*

**Serving Suggestions:** *Serve with Jasmine Rice (page 53). If desired, you can top each serving with Crispy Fried Shallots (page 235) or a dollop of Roasted Chili Paste (Nam Prik Pao, page 240 or store-bought).*

**Variations:** *In Thailand, this dish is usually made with pork and pak boong, also known as ong choy, morning glory, or water spinach. It's my favorite vegetable, but since it's hard to find, this recipe—and many restaurants—substitutes spinach. You can use 1 pound poached pork or chicken breast in place of the tofu (follow the directions in the Chicken and Napa Cabbage Salad with Crispy Shallots, page 106, slicing the poached meat instead of shredding it). You could also use any meat left over from making Basic Thai Chicken Stock (page 91). In place of the spinach, you can use 3 cups broccoli florets, blanched in boiling water until bright green but still crisp, 1 to 2 minutes, and then rinsed in cold water.*

# CHAPTER SEVEN

# Seafood

Seafood is abundant and very popular in Thailand, especially in coastal areas, with freshwater fish such as catfish more prevalent inland. Even dishes that might appear to have no relation to seafood whatsoever very likely contain some, since fish sauce and shrimp paste are used to season so many things.

Fish are usually cooked whole in Thailand, which helps retain moisture and flavor, but in the interest of speed and convenience, I've called for boneless, skinless fillets in this book.

Grilling over charcoal, steaming, and stir-frying are common ways of cooking seafood, and there are also classic soups such as Tom Yum (page 93) and curries, including water-based sour curry (gaeng som) and rich, coconut-y Choo Chee Curry (page 140) that are typically made with seafood.

Shrimp, in particular, either dried or fresh, appear in a great many dishes in a supporting role, such as Bean Thread Noodle Salad (page 101), Green Papaya Salad (page 99), and Pad Thai (page 72).

# POACHED FISH FILLETS IN CHILI, GARLIC, AND LIME SAUCE

## Pla Tun Manow

SPICE LEVEL: MEDIUM

PREP TIME: 5 MINUTES · COOK TIME: ABOUT 15 MINUTES

GLUTEN-FREE · SOY-FREE · NUT-FREE

This dish is quite simple—but the combination of delicate, flaky fish and a bright, zingy chili-lime sauce (often called simply "seafood sauce" because it pairs so well with it) is anything but plain. This dish is usually made with a whole steamed fish, but for a hassle-free home version, I've used fillets and poaching—a gentle, practically foolproof method that keeps the fish moist and tender while infusing it with flavor. Speedy and fuss-free, this makes a great healthy meal when served with a stir-fry vegetable dish and some Jasmine Rice (page 53). SERVES 4

3½ cups water or Basic Thai Chicken Stock (page 91)

2 tablespoons fish sauce

1 lemongrass stalk (bottom 3 inches only, bruised with a pestle or the side of a chef's knife)

2 thin slices ginger (about ¼ inch thick), bruised with a pestle or the side of a chef's knife

1 shallot, diced

1 garlic clove, thinly sliced

4 boneless, skinless fish fillets (about 6 ounces each)

Chili, Garlic, and Lime Sauce (page 236), for serving

¼ cup fresh cilantro leaves, roughly chopped

1. In a sauté pan large enough to hold all 4 fillets over high heat, bring the water, fish sauce, lemongrass, ginger, shallot, and garlic to a boil. When it reaches a boil, turn the heat to low, cover, and simmer for 5 minutes to infuse the water with the aromatics.

2. Add the fish, cover, and cook at the barest simmer–only a few bubbles should be visible–until the fish is opaque on the outside but still slightly translucent inside (it will continue cooking for a few minutes after removed from the pan), 5 to 10 minutes, depending on type of fish and thickness of fillets.

3. Remove the fillets from the poaching liquid with a spatula, and serve with the Chili, Garlic, and Lime Sauce spooned on top and sprinkled with the cilantro.

**Ingredient Tip:** You can use any type of firm, sturdy fish, such as salmon, cod, halibut, or tuna, or shellfish such as shrimp.

**Recipe Tip:** If poaching salmon, you can brine the fillets in 2 tablespoons salt dissolved in 2 cups water for 10 minutes before poaching to minimize the appearance of coagulated white albumin on their surface during cooking.

**Simple Swap:** This dish is also delicious with Sweet Chili Sauce (page 239) in place of the Chile Garlic, and Lime Sauce.

# GRILLED SQUID

### Plamehrk Yang

SPICE LEVEL: MEDIUM

PREP TIME: 5 MINUTES, PLUS 30 MINUTES TO MARINATE · COOK TIME: 5 MINUTES

GLUTEN-FREE · SOY-FREE · NUT-FREE

This is one of my favorite foods, and just the thought of it transports me back to the Thai seaside–sweet squid grilled over charcoal just until crisp on the outside and tender inside, slightly chewy and faintly smoky. Though it's simple and easy to make, the tangy Chili, Garlic, and Lime Sauce (page 236) makes it something truly special. The key to keeping squid tender is to cook it either very quickly over very high heat or gently for a long time; here, we're aiming for fast and hot. **SERVES 4**

4 fresh or frozen squid steaks (calamari steaks), about 6 ounces each (see Note)

1 cup coconut milk

3 tablespoons fish sauce

Chili, Garlic, and Lime Sauce (page 236), for serving

1. With a sharp knife, lightly score both sides of each steak in a diamond hatch pattern to prevent them from curling up while cooking.

2. In a large bowl, mix together the coconut milk and fish sauce, and add the squid steaks. Marinate the steaks for at least 30 minutes (and up to 2 hours).

3. Prepare an oiled charcoal or gas grill or an oiled stovetop grill pan over high heat until very hot.

4. Grill the steaks just until opaque, with grill marks, 1 to 3 minutes per side.

5. Serve immediately with the Chile, Garlic, and Lime Sauce for dipping.

**Note:** Defrost frozen squid steaks overnight in the refrigerator or place them in a resealable plastic bag, submerge the bag in cold water, and defrost for 4 hours at room temperature.

**Ingredient Tip:** This recipe uses "squid steaks," also known as calamari steaks, jumbo squid, or calamari grande fillets, for convenience and even cooking. They are simply flat, rectangular pieces cut from very large squid, about ¼ to ½ inch thick.

**Recipe Tip:** To make these into a street-style finger food, as they would be eaten in Thailand, cut the scored, oiled, and seasoned steaks into smaller pieces and thread them onto bamboo skewers (soaked in cold water for 30 minutes prior to grilling to prevent burning).

**Leftover Tip:** If you have any leftover grilled squid, cut it into bite-size pieces and toss it in the dressing for Grilled Steak Salad (page 114) with tomatoes, lettuce, thinly sliced shallots, and fresh cilantro leaves to make a Thai-style seafood salad.

**Simple Swap:** Try the same technique with calamari or octopus.

# GREEN CURRY MUSSELS

### *Gaeng Kiew Wan Hoy Malaeng Pu*

SPICE LEVEL: MEDIUM

PREP TIME: 10 MINUTES · COOK TIME: 15 MINUTES

GLUTEN-FREE · SOY-FREE · NUT-FREE

This quick-and-easy, yet elegant, fusion dish joins fragrant green curry flavors and creamy coconut milk with a Belgian-style method for cooking mussels. If you've never cooked mussels before, don't be intimidated–they're not difficult to clean or cook, and they're ready in no time. For a milder dish, use just 1 tablespoon curry paste. This would be an impressive, yet low-effort, dinner-party dish. It's even better with homemade green curry paste. **SERVES 3 TO 4**

2 pounds mussels

1 tablespoon vegetable oil

1 garlic clove, minced

2 tablespoons Green Curry Paste
(page 132 or store-bought)

1 (14-ounce) can coconut milk, divided

1 tablespoon fish sauce

1 lemongrass stalk, bottom 3 inches only, bruised with a pestle or the side of a chef's knife

Lime wedges, for serving

Fresh cilantro leaves, roughly chopped, for serving

2 kaffir lime leaves, very thinly sliced (chiffonade; see Ingredient Tip; optional)

1. Clean the mussels thoroughly, scrubbing them under cold running water with a stiff brush and removing any beards by pulling them off with your fingers.

2. In a large pot or Dutch oven over medium heat, heat the oil. Add the garlic, and cook until fragrant, 30 seconds to 1 minute.

3. Add the curry paste and 3 tablespoons of the coconut cream from the top of the can (if there's no cream, just use the coconut milk), stirring with a wooden spoon, until fragrant and slightly thickened, 2 to 3 minutes.

4. Add the remaining coconut milk and the fish sauce and lemongrass. Bring to a simmer, turn the heat to low, and simmer, covered, for 4 minutes.

5. Add the mussels, stir, cover, and cook until all the mussels are opened, 5 to 8 minutes, stirring every minute or so.

6. Distribute the mussels and curry broth among shallow bowls (discarding any mussels that didn't open), and serve with lime wedges, sprinkling each serving with cilantro and chiffonade of kaffir lime leaf (if using).

**Ingredient tip:** *To chiffonade the kaffir lime leaves (if using): Stack them on top of each other, roll them up tightly, and slice as thinly as possible.*

# SPICY STIR-FRIED SHRIMP WITH ROASTED CHILI PASTE

## *Goong Pad Nam Prik Pao*

SPICE LEVEL: MEDIUM

PREP TIME: 15 MINUTES · COOK TIME: 5 MINUTES

GLUTEN-FREE · SOY-FREE · NUT-FREE

This is an easy, lightning-fast stir-fry that's bursting with flavor from the roasted chili paste (*nam prik pao*), also known as "chili jam." It's the same paste used to season Tom Yum Soup (page 93). If you use store-bought chili paste (often labeled as "Chili Paste in Soybean Oil"), it often comes in mild, medium, and hot varieties, so you can pick your spice level. This stir-fry can also be made with mussels, clams, scallops, calamari, fish, or any other seafood, as well as bite-size pieces of any kind of meat or tofu. **SERVES 3 TO 4**

1 pound fresh or frozen raw shell-on shrimp (see Note)

3 tablespoons Roasted Chili Paste (page 240 or store-bought)

2 tablespoons fish sauce

¼ cup water or Basic Thai Chicken Stock (page 91)

1 teaspoon palm sugar, light brown sugar, or granulated sugar (omit if using homemade chili paste)

2 tablespoons vegetable oil

1 tablespoon minced garlic (about 2 large cloves)

2 scallions, cut into 2-inch lengths, white parts also halved lengthwise, kept separate

2 fresh red Thai bird's-eye, jalapeño, or serrano chiles, stemmed and quartered lengthwise into thin slices (optional)

Jasmine Rice (page 53), for serving

1.  Peel and devein the shrimp, leaving the tails on. Set aside.

2.  In a small bowl, stir to mix the chili paste, fish sauce, water, and sugar until the sugar dissolves. Set aside.

3.  In a large wok or skillet over medium heat, heat the oil.

4.  Add the garlic and scallion whites, and stir-fry just until fragrant, about 30 seconds.

5.  Add the shrimp, and stir-fry just until they turn pink, 2 to 3 minutes.

6.  Add the sauce and the chiles (if using), and stir-fry for 1 minute longer.

7.  Turn off the heat, add the scallion greens, and stir a few times, until the scallion greens are slightly softened.

8.  Serve immediately with Jasmine Rice.

**Note:** *Defrost frozen shrimp overnight in the refrigerator or place them in a resealable plastic bag, submerge the bag in cold water, and defrost for about 2 hours at room temperature if frozen in a block, 20 to 30 minutes if frozen individually.*

**Serving Suggestion:** *Serve topped with fresh cilantro leaves and fresh lime wedges for squeezing over individual servings.*

# STIR-FRIED YELLOW CURRY CRAB

### Bpoo Pad Pong Garee

SPICE LEVEL: NONE

PREP TIME: 10 MINUTES · COOK TIME: ABOUT 5 MINUTES

NUT-FREE

This is a sit down–restaurant type of dish, rather than street food. Many times, when my extended family had reunions in Bangkok, we'd convene in a bustling restaurant and devour large quantities of this delicious crab stir-fried with mild yellow curry powder. It's typically made with whole crabs, but for a streamlined home version that's less messy to cook and eat, this recipe calls for precooked crab meat. SERVES 4

1 tablespoon fish sauce

1 tablespoon oyster sauce

¼ teaspoon palm sugar or granulated sugar

¼ teaspoon ground white or black pepper

3 tablespoons vegetable oil

1 tablespoon minced garlic (about 2 large cloves)

½ small onion, cut into ½-inch wedges

2 scallions, cut into 2-inch lengths, white parts also halved lengthwise, kept separate

1 or 2 fresh Thai bird's-eye, jalapeño, or serrano chiles, stemmed and quartered lengthwise into thin slices (optional)

¾ pound fresh or frozen cooked crab meat in large chunks (see Note)

1 tablespoon curry powder

½ cup roughly chopped thin stems and leaves from the top of 1 or 2 celery stalks

2 eggs, lightly beaten

2 tablespoons milk, coconut milk, Basic Thai Chicken Stock (page 91), or water, if needed

Jasmine Rice (page 53), for serving

1. In a small bowl, mix the fish sauce, oyster sauce, sugar, and pepper, and set aside.

2. In a large wok or skillet over medium heat, heat the oil. Add the garlic, onion, and scallion whites, and stir-fry for 1 minute.

3. Add the chiles (if using), and stir-fry for 30 seconds.

4. Add the crab, curry powder, celery, and sauce, and stir-fry very gently (so as not to break the pieces of crab) until evenly combined.

5. Add the eggs, and gently mix into the other ingredients, continuing to stir-fry until the egg firms up, scraping the bottom of the wok with a wooden spoon or spatula to prevent the egg from sticking, about 2 minutes longer. The egg will be incorporated into the sauce, but if it looks slightly scrambled, don't worry; that's normal. If the sauce seems too dry at this point, you can add the milk.

6. Add the scallion greens, and stir-fry until they are slightly softened, about 30 seconds.

7. Serve immediately with Jasmine Rice.

**Note:** *Defrost frozen crabmeat overnight in the refrigerator or place in a resealable plastic bag, submerge the bag in cold water, and defrost for 3 to 4 hours at room temperature. Make sure the meat is well-drained before using it in the recipe.*

**Variations:** *To make it with whole crabs, use approximately 1½ pounds of crabs, cut into quarters. You can also make it with crab legs or claws, lobster, large shell-on shrimp, scallops, or bite-size pieces of fish, chicken, or pork. Add 1 ounce of bean thread/glass noodles, previously soaked in warm water for 15 minutes, after the egg is cooked, and stir-fry until softened, 1 to 2 minutes, to make it into a one-dish meal.*

# SPICY RED CURRY STIR-FRIED SCALLOPS WITH BASIL

## *Pad Pehd Hoy Scallop*

SPICE LEVEL: HOT

PREP TIME: 5 MINUTES · COOK TIME: ABOUT 10 MINUTES

GLUTEN-FREE · SOY-FREE · NUT-FREE

This intensely flavored dish is like a drier curry that's stir-fried rather than simmered. It's typically made with bite-size pieces of fish that have been deep-fried until very crunchy, but this quicker, healthier version uses firm scallops instead. The young green peppercorns, available either fresh or in glass jars in Asian markets, add a wonderful fragrance and piquant spice; the peppercorns are edible, but the stems are not. **SERVES 3 TO 4**

2 tablespoons vegetable oil

2 tablespoons Red Curry Paste (page 130 or store-bought)

¼ cup water or Basic Thai Chicken Stock (page 91)

1 tablespoon fish sauce

1 tablespoon palm sugar, light brown sugar, or granulated sugar

2 stems young green peppercorns, fresh or brined (optional but recommended)

1 pound fresh or frozen scallops (see Note)

½ cup fresh Thai sweet basil or Italian sweet basil leaves

Jasmine Rice (page 53), for serving

1. In a large wok or skillet over medium heat, heat the oil.

2. Add the curry paste, and cook until slightly thickened, darkened, and fragrant, about 2 minutes.

3. Stir in the water, fish sauce, and sugar, and stir until the sugar dissolves.

4. Add the peppercorns (if using), turn the heat to medium-low, and simmer gently for 2 minutes.

5. Add the scallops, and simmer in the curry sauce just until opaque, 5 to 8 minutes, depending on their size.

6. Turn off the heat, stir in the basil leaves just until wilted, and serve with Jasmine Rice.

**Note:** *Defrost frozen scallops overnight in the refrigerator or place them in a resealable plastic bag, submerge the bag in cold water, and defrost for 3 to 4 hours at room temperature.*

**Serving Suggestion:** *Garnish with fresh or fried basil leaves and julienned fresh kaffir lime leaf just before serving.*

**Variations:** *You can also use crisp-fried pieces of fish in place of the scallops, or bite-size pieces of beef, pork, chicken, or tofu.*

# CHAPTER EIGHT

# Chicken and Eggs

Chicken, together with pork, is one of the most widely used meats in Thai cooking. Curries such as Yellow Curry (page 128), Green Curry (page 132), and Mussamun (page 136) are often made with chicken, as is Chiang Mai's Khao Soi Gai noodle curry (page 85). Chicken is cooked in many other ways, including frying, steaming, stir-frying, or grilling. Thais generally prefer bone-in, skin-on dark meat, which is more flavorful and tender. You can use boneless, skinless chicken breast in any of the recipes, but you will need to adjust the cooking time and cut it into slightly thicker slices to avoid dry results.

In Thailand, eggs are eaten at any time of day, not just at breakfast, and are just as important and popular a protein source as meat or seafood. A Thai-Style Omelet (page 187) is one of the most classic comfort foods, and probably one of the first things that most Thais learn how to cook.

# Pad Kra Pao:
# Holy Basil Stir-Fry

One of Thailand's most popular stir-fries, *pad kra pao* is made with finely minced or ground meat and served with Jasmine Rice (page 53) and topped with a crisp-fried egg. (It can also be made with any meat, seafood, or protein source cut into bite-size pieces, and the egg is optional.)

The odd thing is that many who are big fans of this dish might never have tasted the real deal. "*Kra pao*" (more correctly written and pronounced *ga phrao*) means "holy basil," and the name of the dish means "holy basil stir-fry." It can be applied to any dish stir-fried with holy basil (see page 9). The problem is that holy basil, also known as *tulsi*, is difficult to find in many places. Even many overseas Thai restaurants, unless they're willing and able to grow their own, are forced to use other types of basil, or even mint, as a substitute.

The good news is that it's okay to use Thai sweet basil, *horapa* (see page 9) or Italian sweet basil instead. Your dish will not have quite the same peppery flavor as the original, but it will still be tasty. Technically, when made with sweet basil, the name of the dish becomes *pad horapa*.

Another option is to use store-bought holy basil stir-fry sauce, much easier to find than fresh holy basil. It's sold in Asian markets in small glass jars, usually labeled "Chili Paste with Holy Basil Leaves" (พริกผัดกะเพรา). I always keep some on hand for quick-and-easy, last-minute stir-fries; once opened, it lasts for several months in the refrigerator. I "doctor" the paste by stir-frying 1 tablespoon minced garlic in vegetable oil, adding 1 pound ground or bite-size meat, stir-frying until browned, and then adding 4 to 5 tablespoons of the paste, 3 tablespoons fish sauce, 3 tablespoons oyster sauce (or to taste), and some fresh basil of any type (if I have some). You can do this with any meat, seafood, or tofu and any vegetables you'd like—add some steamed rice, and dinner is served! It's not as good as from-scratch, of course, but it's a great convenient option.

# FRIED EGG SALAD

### Yum Kai Dao

SPICE LEVEL: MILD

PREP TIME: 10 MINUTES · COOK TIME: 5 MINUTES

GLUTEN-FREE · SOY-FREE · NUT-FREE · VEGETARIAN

A salad made with fried eggs might sound odd at first, but the contrast between the crisp-fried eggs; bright, tangy dressing; and cool, crunchy greens is delightful. This recipe describes how to make Thai-style fried eggs, which are deep-fried in oil until crisp and golden brown around the edges. Use the same method to make fried eggs to accompany Stir-Fried Chicken with Basil (page 195). **SERVES 4**

**FOR THE THAI-STYLE CRISP FRIED EGGS**

¼ cup vegetable oil

4 large eggs, at room temperature

**FOR THE DRESSING**

¼ cup freshly squeezed lime juice

3 tablespoons fish sauce

1 tablespoon palm sugar or granulated sugar

1 or 2 fresh Thai bird's-eye chiles or 1 jalapeño or serrano, stemmed and diced

**FOR THE SALAD**

1 cup 2-inch pieces lettuce

1 tomato, cored and cut into 8 wedges

¼ cup thinly sliced shallot

¼ cup grated carrot

¼ cup coarsely chopped celery leaves (optional)

¼ cup coarsely chopped fresh cilantro

2 scallions, dark-green parts only, cut into ¼-inch rings

**TO MAKE THAI-STYLE CRISP-FRIED EGGS**

1. In a large wok or nonstick frying pan over high heat, heat the oil. When the oil is very hot, gently crack the egg into the oil and lower the heat to medium. The egg should puff up and sizzle immediately. (It's best to fry the eggs in batches of 1 or 2 at a time.)

*continued*

2. Fry until the egg is crisp and golden-brown around the edges and the yolk is no longer runny, spooning some of the oil over the top of the eggs to help the yolk set, 1 to 2 minutes. Depending on how you prefer your yolks, you can remove the eggs from the heat at this point or flip them over until the top of the egg is crisp as well, about 30 seconds longer. Remove from the oil with a spatula, and drain on a paper towel–lined plate.

### TO MAKE THE DRESSING AND SALAD

1. In a small bowl, stir all the dressing ingredients together until the sugar is completely dissolved.

2. Cut the eggs into 2- to 3-inch pieces. In a large bowl, toss the egg pieces gently with the dressing, lettuce, tomato, shallot, carrot, celery leaves (if using), cilantro, and scallion. Transfer to a large platter and serve immediately.

**Simple Swap:** *You can make a similar salad using peeled and quartered hard-boiled eggs instead of the fried egg.*

**Recipe Tip:** *This recipe makes a Thai-style protein-heavy salad. To make it more Western-style, double the amounts of lettuce, celery leaves (if using), and tomatoes.*

# THAI-STYLE OMELET

*Kai Jiew*

SPICE LEVEL: NONE

PREP TIME: 5 MINUTES · COOK TIME: 5 MINUTES

NUT-FREE

Perhaps the ultimate Thai comfort food, this home-style dish is one that you'll rarely find in restaurants outside of Thailand. Add rice and it's a great weeknight meal that's ready in less than 15 minutes. It's basically the opposite of a classic French omelet, so forget all the rules you've been taught for making soft, tender omelets cooked over low, gentle heat. A Thai omelet is cooked in very hot oil over high heat and should puff up immediately when the eggs hit the oil, and then it's fried till crisp and browned. This recipe is for a plain omelet, but it's often made with ground pork (see Variations).

**SERVES 4**

4 eggs, at room temperature

4 teaspoons fish sauce or soy sauce

Pinch ground white pepper (optional)

1 tablespoon thinly sliced scallion (optional)

1 tablespoon chopped fresh cilantro (optional)

¼ cup vegetable oil

1. Break the eggs into a medium bowl, and whisk in the fish sauce, pepper, scallion (if using), and cilantro (if using) briskly with a fork until the mixture is well-combined, airy, and foamy.

2. In a large, well-seasoned wok or nonstick skillet over high heat, heat the oil until very hot. You can test to see if it's hot enough by letting just a drop of the egg mixture fall into the oil from the tines of the fork. If the drop sizzles and puffs up as soon as it hits the oil, the oil is ready.

3. Pour the egg into the oil (it should puff up immediately), and use a fork to pull the edges of the omelet toward the middle so that all of the egg touches the hot oil and cooks evenly. Fry until golden-brown and crisp on both sides, 1½ to 2 minutes per side, flipping the omelet halfway through. You can use the edge of a spatula to break the omelet into halves or quarters to make it easier to flip, if necessary.

*continued*

4.  Using a metal spatula, transfer the omelet to a paper towel–lined plate and drain briefly, and then transfer to a serving plate and serve hot. The omelet will deflate once removed from the pan, but don't worry; that's normal.

**Serving Suggestions:** *This omelet is traditionally eaten over fluffy Jasmine Rice (page 53), drizzled with a bit of Sriracha sauce.*

**Recipe Note:** *I usually make 2-egg omelets, with 2 to 3 teaspoons fish sauce. It's difficult to make this with fewer than 2 eggs or more than 4, but 2 to 3 eggs work fine for most woks and 10- to 12-inch skillets.*

**Variations:** *I like to make mine with a bit of cilantro, but many people add some chopped scallion. You can use both, one or the other, or neither, as you wish. I also usually whisk in 3 ounces of ground pork (or any other ground meat) at the same time as the fish sauce, pepper, and cilantro. You can add mussels or oysters, or any other quick-cooking protein. These omelets are also a great way to use up leftover stir-fry or fried rice.*

# SON-IN-LAW FRIED HARDBOILED EGGS IN TAMARIND SAUCE

*Kai Look Keuy*

SPICE LEVEL: MILD

PREP TIME: 10 MINUTES · COOK TIME: 15 MINUTES

GLUTEN-FREE · SOY-FREE · NUT-FREE

Yet another Thai dish with a puzzling name for which there is no definitive explanation, Son-in-Law Eggs are hardboiled and then fried till crisp around the edges, cut into halves or wedges, and topped with a tangy sweet-and-sour tamarind sauce and Crispy Fried Shallots (page 235). The combination might sound as bizarre as the name, but it's addictively tasty. This is a great way to use up leftover hardboiled eggs—for example, after Easter. **SERVES 4**

6 large eggs

¼ cup palm sugar or light brown sugar

2 tablespoons tamarind paste (see page 26 or store-bought)

2 tablespoons fish sauce

2 tablespoons water

Neutral vegetable oil, for frying

¼ cup Crispy Fried Shallots (page 235), for serving

2 tablespoons fresh cilantro leaves, for serving (optional)

4 roasted or fried chiles or ¼ teaspoon Ground Roasted Chili Powder (page 230), for serving (optional; see Note)

1. In a medium pot, cover the eggs with cold water by 1 inch. Bring to a boil over medium-high heat. As soon as the water reaches a rolling boil, turn off the heat, cover the pot, and let sit for 10 minutes.

2. While the eggs are sitting, make the sauce: In a small saucepan over medium-low heat, heat the palm sugar, tamarind paste, fish sauce, and water. Stir until the sugar is dissolved, and then simmer until slightly thickened, about 5 minutes. It should be about the consistency of maple syrup. Taste and adjust the seasoning, as necessary, for an equal sweet-sour-salty balance.

*continued*

3.  When the 10 minutes are up, carefully drain off the hot water from the eggs and fill the pot with enough cold water to cover the eggs. Let sit until the eggs are cool enough to handle, and then peel: Rap each egg a few times on a counter to crack the shell, and then gently roll the egg on the countertop or squeeze it gently in your hand to crack the shell all over, and peel the shell off. Pat the eggs dry with a paper towel.

4.  In a wok or small skillet over medium-high heat, heat about 1 inch of oil, and then add the eggs, turning them until bubbly crisp and golden-brown all over, 5 to 6 minutes. Be careful because the eggs might spatter while frying; use a splatter guard, if necessary.

5.  Remove the eggs from the pan with a slotted spoon or mesh skimmer, and drain them on a paper towel–lined plate. When cool enough to handle, cut them lengthwise into halves or quarters, and arrange them on a serving plate. Drizzle with the sauce; garnish with the Crispy Fried Shallots, cilantro (if using), and chiles (if using); and serve.

> **Note:** To make roasted chiles, toast 4 dried red chiles in a small dry skillet over medium heat until fragrant and slightly browned, 1 to 2 minutes. To make fried chiles, add 4 dried red chiles to the hot oil after removing the fried eggs and fry until fragrant and browned, 30 seconds to 1 minute. Alternatively, you can sprinkle a bit of Ground Roasted Chili Powder (page 230) on top of the eggs when serving.
>
> **Vegetarian Version:** Use soy sauce in place of the fish sauce.

# STIR-FRIED GINGER CHICKEN

### Gai Pad Khing

PREP TIME: 10 MINUTES, PLUS 10 MINUTES TO SOAK
AND MARINATE · COOK TIME: 10 MINUTES

NUT-FREE

Ginger, contrary to popular belief, is not used often in Thai cooking and appears only in strongly Chinese-influenced dishes, such as this mild stir-fry. If you can find young ginger, available in Asian grocery stores, it has a milder taste, doesn't require peeling, and is easier to cut, but regular mature ginger works fine—just be sure to cut it into a very fine julienne. **SERVES 4**

½ cup dried cloud-ear or wood-ear mushroom (see Note)

2 tablespoons soy sauce

2 tablespoons fish sauce

1 tablespoon oyster sauce

½ teaspoon palm sugar or granulated sugar

1 pound boneless, skinless chicken (breast or thigh), cut against the grain into bite-size pieces about ¼-inch thick

2 tablespoons vegetable oil

2 tablespoons minced garlic (3 or 4 large cloves)

1 cup grated carrot

½ cup sliced red bell pepper

1 (3-inch) piece ginger, peeled and finely julienned into very thin matchsticks

4 scallions, cut into 2-inch lengths, white parts also halved lengthwise

½ teaspoon sesame oil (optional)

Pinch ground white pepper or black pepper (optional)

Jasmine Rice (page 53), for serving

1.  In a medium bowl, soak the mushrooms in enough warm water to cover until softened, about 10 minutes.

2.  Meanwhile, in another medium bowl, mix the soy sauce, fish sauce, oyster sauce, and sugar. Add the chicken pieces, and toss to coat evenly. Marinate in the refrigerator for 5 to 10 minutes.

3.  Rinse and drain the mushrooms well, and cut them into bite-size slices. Set aside.

*continued*

4. In a large wok or skillet over medium heat, heat the vegetable oil until shimmering. Add the garlic, and stir-fry just until light golden, 30 seconds to 1 minute.

5. Add the chicken and sauce mixture, and stir-fry until no longer pink, 4 to 5 minutes.

6. Add the mushrooms, carrot, bell pepper, ginger, scallions, and sesame oil (if using), and stir-fry just until the vegetables are softened but still crisp-tender, another 1 to 2 minutes.

7. Sprinkle with the pepper (if using), and serve with Jasmine Rice.

**Note:** *This dish is typically made with dried cloud-ear mushrooms (known as black fungus or black fungus with white back, Auricularia polytricha) or wood-ear (known as Jew's ear or black fungus, Auricularia auricula-judae) mushrooms, but you can use any mild-flavored dried or fresh mushroom, or omit them if you're not a mushroom fan. For fresh mushrooms, use 1½ to 2 cups sliced fresh button, cremini, or any other fresh mushroom, and add at the same time as the carrot and ginger.*

**Dial Up the Heat:** *This dish is naturally quite mild, but you can add 1 or 2 fresh red Thai bird's-eye, jalapeño, or serrano chiles at the same time as the mushrooms, carrot, and ginger for a slightly spicier dish. Or you can add 1 cup thinly sliced red bell pepper for a bit of color without any spice.*

# STIR-FRIED CASHEW CHICKEN

### Gai Pad Mehd Mamuang Himmapun

SPICE LEVEL: MILD

PREP TIME: 10 MINUTES, PLUS 10 MINUTES TO MARINATE · COOK TIME: 5 MINUTES

Another Thai stir-fry of Chinese origin, this one is similar to the famous Sichuan dish Kung Pao, but with cashew nuts instead of peanuts. The meat is often breaded and fried separately before cooking together with the sauce and other ingredients, but this streamlined, healthier method cuts out those extra steps. Because the chiles are kept whole and added at the last minute, the dish is quite mild, despite its appearance, but you can reduce or omit the chiles, if you prefer. **SERVES 4**

1 tablespoon soy sauce plus 4 teaspoons, divided

¼ teaspoon baking soda

1 pound boneless, skinless chicken (breast or thigh), cut against the grain into bite-size pieces about ¼-inch thick

¼ cup oyster sauce

½ teaspoon sesame oil

1 teaspoon palm sugar or granulated sugar

2 tablespoons vegetable oil

6 to 8 (2- to 3-inch-long) dried red chiles, stemmed (optional)

2 tablespoons minced garlic (3 or 4 large cloves)

½ medium onion, cut into ¼-inch slices

4 scallions, cut into 2-inch lengths, white parts also halved lengthwise, kept separate

½ cup roasted cashew nuts

Jasmine Rice (page 53), for serving

1. In a medium bowl, mix 1 tablespoon of the soy sauce with the baking soda. Add the chicken pieces, toss to coat evenly, and transfer to the refrigerator to marinate and tenderize for 10 minutes.

2. Meanwhile, in a small bowl, mix the oyster sauce, remaining 4 teaspoons soy sauce, sesame oil, and sugar. Stir until the sugar is dissolved, and set aside.

3. In a large wok or skillet over medium heat, heat the oil until shimmering. Add the chiles (if using), and stir-fry just until fragrant and slightly browned, but not blackened, 15 to 30 seconds. Remove the chiles from the oil using a slotted spoon, mesh skimmer, or mesh spider, and set aside.

*continued*

4. Add the garlic to the hot oil, and stir-fry for 30 seconds. Add the chicken, and stir-fry until browned, about 3 minutes. Add the onion and scallion whites, and stir-fry until crisp-tender, about 1 minute.

5. Add the sauce mixture, scallion greens, cashews, and fried chiles, and stir-fry just until all the ingredients are evenly coated in the sauce and the scallion greens are slightly softened, 30 seconds to 1 minute.

6. Serve immediately with Jasmine Rice.

**Ingredient Tip:** You can use either salted or unsalted cashews; if using salted nuts, just adjust the seasoning of the sauce, as necessary, or rinse them before use.

# STIR-FRIED CHICKEN WITH BASIL

## Pad Ga Phrao Gai

SPICE LEVEL: MEDIUM

PREP TIME: 5 MINUTES · COOK TIME: 5 MINUTES

NUT-FREE

One of Thailand's most popular stir-fries, this is often served as a one-dish meal with steamed rice and topped with a crisp-fried egg. It's incredibly quick and easy to make, great for a busy weekday lunch or dinner. You can use any type of basil in this dish, since peppery holy basil is hard to find. Traditionalists don't use any soy sauce or oyster sauce in this dish, seasoning only with fish sauce, but these days most people add them for flavor, color, and a hint of sweetness. **SERVES 4**

6 garlic cloves

6 fresh red Thai bird's-eye chiles (or to taste), stemmed

2 tablespoons fish sauce

2 tablespoons soy sauce

1 tablespoon dark sweet soy sauce (aka "black sweet soy sauce"; see page 8)

1 tablespoon oyster sauce

2 tablespoons vegetable oil

1 pound ground or finely minced chicken

1 tablespoon water, if needed

1½ cups fresh basil leaves (holy, Thai sweet, or Italian sweet)

1. If using a mortar and pestle, finely chop the garlic and chiles, and then pound them together to form a coarse paste. Otherwise, finely mince both.

2. In a small bowl, mix the fish sauce, soy sauces, and oyster sauce together, and set aside.

3. In a large wok or skillet over medium heat, heat the oil. Add the garlic-chili paste (or finely minced garlic and chiles), and fry just until fragrant, about 30 seconds.

4. Add the chicken, and cook, stirring with a wooden spoon or spatula to break it up into smaller pieces, until browned, 2 to 3 minutes.

*continued*

5. Add the sauce mixture, and stir-fry for about 2 minutes longer. You can add the water if the mixture is too dry.

6. Turn off the heat, add the basil leaves, and stir just until the basil is wilted. Serve immediately.

**Serving Suggestion:** Serve with Jasmine Rice (page 53), a crisp-fried egg (follow the steps for making Thai-Style Crisp-Fried Eggs in the recipe for Fried Egg Salad, page 185), cucumber slices, and some Spicy Fish Sauce (page 233).

**Simple Swaps:** You can also use ground turkey, beef, or pork, or any meat or tofu cut into bite-size pieces.

**Optional Additions:** You can also add ½ onion cut into ¼-inch slices, thinly sliced bell pepper, or green beans cut into 2-inch pieces.

**Ingredient Tip:** You can use store-bought ground meat, use a food processor to coarsely grind it, or finely mince your own with a chef's knife (for the best texture).

# FIVE SPICE-BRAISED CHICKEN AND EGGS

*Kai Pa-Lo*

SPICE LEVEL: NONE

PREP TIME: 10 MINUTES, PLUS 20 MINUTES TO REST · COOK TIME: 25 MINUTES

NUT-FREE

This is a Thai-Chinese comfort classic: chicken (or pork) braised with hardboiled eggs in a mild, fragrant five-spice sauce. The meat stays tender and juicy, and the eggs are colored brown by the soy sauce and infused with the warm spices. You can use any five-spice powder (available in most large supermarkets as well as Asian markets); they vary widely and—despite the name—often contain more than five of any of the following: cinnamon, coriander, fennel, star anise, orange peel, licorice, Sichuan peppercorn, black pepper, cloves, bay leaves, or allspice. The sauce is thin but flavorful, and the dish should be served with plenty of steamed rice, not served as a soup.

**SERVES 4**

1 pound bone-in, skin-on chicken legs and/or thighs

1 tablespoon five-spice powder

1 tablespoon vegetable oil

1 tablespoon minced garlic

4 cups water or Basic Thai Chicken Stock (page 91)

3 tablespoons palm sugar or light brown sugar or granulated sugar

2 tablespoons dark sweet soy sauce (aka "black sweet soy sauce"; see page 8)

2 tablespoons soy sauce

1 teaspoon salt

½ teaspoon ground white pepper or black pepper

4 hardboiled eggs (see Note)

8 fried tofu cubes (optional; see Note)

2 tablespoons coarsely chopped fresh cilantro leaves, for serving

Jasmine Rice (page 53), for serving

*continued*

1.   On a platter, sprinkle the chicken pieces with the five-spice powder, and rub the spice into the chicken using your hands. Transfer the chicken to the refrigerator to rest for 20 minutes.

2.   In a medium saucepan over medium heat, heat the oil. Add the garlic, and sauté until fragrant, about 20 seconds.

3.   Add the chicken pieces and cook, turning frequently with tongs, until evenly browned all over, about 5 minutes.

4.   Add the water, sugar, soy sauces, salt, and pepper, and stir until the sugar and salt are dissolved.

5.   Add the hardboiled eggs and tofu (if using), cover, raise the heat to medium-high to bring to a boil, and then turn the heat to low and simmer, covered, for 20 minutes. Before serving with cilantro and Jasmine Rice, remove the eggs from the pot, cut them in half lengthwise, and return them to the pot.

**Note:** *To make the hardboiled eggs, follow steps 1 and 3 in Son-in-Law Fried Hardboiled Eggs (page 189). You can make the hardboiled eggs while the chicken rests in step 1.*

**Ingredient Tip:** *Fried pieces of tofu (usually about 1½ inches to 2 inches square) are sold in Asian markets in the refrigerated section, with all the other types of tofu. They have a somewhat spongy texture inside that is great for soaking up sauces. If you can't find them, you can use firm or extra-firm tofu cut into 2-by-2-by-1-inch pieces, or simply omit the tofu.*

**Ingredient Tip:** *If you can't find dark sweet soy sauce (aka "black sweet soy sauce"; see page 8), you can use 3 tablespoons regular soy sauce and add 1 teaspoon molasses, or simply increase the amount of sugar, as necessary.*

**Variations:** *This dish is most often made with chicken or pork (you could use large chunks of pork butt, shoulder, or pork belly), but you can also use beef, duck, or meatballs. For a vegetarian version, omit the chicken and use only tofu and eggs, or just eggs, increasing the number to 8.*

# GRILLED GARLIC-LEMONGRASS CHICKEN

## Gai Yang

SPICE LEVEL: NONE

PREP TIME: 10 MINUTES, PLUS 30 MINUTES TO MARINATE ·
COOK TIME: 25 MINUTES, PLUS 10 MINUTES TO REST

NUT-FREE

A classic from the northeastern Isaan region, this flavorful favorite is usually made with split-open whole birds grilled over hot coals and served with Sticky Rice (page 55), Green Papaya Salad (page 99), and Sweet Chili Sauce (page 239) topped with coarsely chopped fresh cilantro. Some variations add turmeric to the marinade, but this version is flavored with lemongrass in addition to the "three pals" of garlic, cilantro, and pepper (see page 9). **SERVES 4**

3 tablespoons finely chopped garlic (2 or 3 large cloves)

2 tablespoons finely chopped cilantro roots or stems

1 tablespoon finely chopped lemongrass (from the bottom 3 inches of 1 or 2 stalks; see page 12)

1 teaspoon white or black peppercorns

Pinch salt

¼ cup coconut milk

2 tablespoons soy sauce

2 tablespoons fish sauce

2 tablespoons palm sugar or brown sugar

2½ pounds bone-in, skin-on chicken thighs and legs

1. In a mortar and pestle or blender or using an immersion blender, pound or blend the garlic, cilantro roots or stems, lemongrass, peppercorns, and salt to form a paste.

2. In a small bowl, mix the paste with the coconut milk, soy sauce, fish sauce, and sugar, stirring until the sugar dissolves.

3.  Arrange the chicken in a shallow baking dish or bowl, and add the marinade, turning the chicken so that all sides of each piece are evenly covered in marinade. Cover with plastic wrap, and transfer to the refrigerator to marinate for at least 30 minutes (and up to overnight), turning the pieces occasionally so that they marinate evenly.

4.  Grill on an oiled charcoal or gas grill on medium-high heat or on an oiled stove-top grill pan over medium heat until cooked through (165°F on an instant-read thermometer), 20 to 25 minutes.

5.  Let rest for 10 minutes before serving.

**Recipe Tip:** *If you don't have a grill or grill pan, you can also bake the chicken in a 450°F oven for 20 to 25 minutes on a roasting rack placed above a foil-lined baking sheet.*

# CHAPTER NINE

# Beef and Pork

Beef is expensive in Thailand, and many Thai Buddhists do not eat beef for religious reasons (disciples of the Goddess of Mercy, Jao Mae Guan Im, known as Kwan Yin in Chinese, are forbidden from eating it). It therefore appears in far fewer traditional Thai recipes than pork and chicken, and many of those dishes are Thai Muslim dishes, such as Mussamun Curry (page 154).

Pork, on the other hand, is very popular in Thailand and is probably the most commonly used meat, together with chicken. Most Thai curries, grilled specialties, and stir-fry dishes usually feature pork or chicken, and often dark-meat cuts.

That said, the dishes in this chapter—and most Thai dishes in general—can be made with any meat, seafood, or meat alternative that you prefer, adjusting as necessary for cooking time.

# "Velveting" Meat for Tender Texture

Any Thai dish that is stir-fried—including popular noodle dishes such as Pad Thai—has Chinese origins, since the cooking technique was introduced to Thailand by Chinese immigrants. The use of Chinese ingredients such as soy sauce and oyster sauce in many Thai stir-fries also hints at their heritage. In some of these stir-fry recipes, I've taken this connection a step further by using a modified take on another Chinese cooking technique, called "velveting," employed by many Chinese restaurants to ensure a silky, tender texture in stir-fried meats.

Typically, thinly sliced meat is marinated in a mixture of cornstarch, rice wine, and egg white, and then blanched in hot oil or water, which alters the pH on the surface of the meat so that it remains moist and incredibly tender when cooked. Briefly soaking the sliced meat in a simple water-and-baking soda solution, however, has the same effect, while requiring fewer ingredients and omitting a cumbersome blanching step.

The treated meat does need to be rinsed before cooking, however, to remove any trace of baking soda, which can affect the taste and texture of the final dish if not rinsed off. If you've ever wondered how your favorite takeout place achieves such a velvety-soft texture in their stir-fried meats, give velveting a try! You can use it with any type of meat, and it's not limited to stir-frying either—you can velvet any sliced meat before deep-frying or simmering as well. It's particularly useful for tougher cuts or for lean meats that tend to dry out quickly, such as chicken breast.

# CRYING TIGER GRILLED STEAK

*Suea Rong Hai*

SPICE LEVEL: MEDIUM

PREP TIME: 5 MINUTES, PLUS 30 MINUTES TO MARINATE
COOK TIME: 5 TO 10 MINUTES, PLUS 10 MINUTES TO REST

NUT-FREE

Nobody really knows why the tiger is crying (perhaps the sauce is too spicy for him?), but this popular classic from the northeastern Isaan region is delicious and a quick-and-easy way to make grilled steak far more exciting. It is the sauce that makes this Crying Tiger (without it, this is simply grilled beef, or *nuea yang*), and it's normally served with steamed Sticky Rice (page 55), though it's also good with Jasmine Rice (page 53). **SERVES 4**

2 tablespoons soy sauce

2 tablespoons minced garlic (3 or 4 large cloves)

1 tablespoon fish sauce

2 teaspoons palm sugar, light brown sugar, or granulated sugar

⅛ teaspoon ground white pepper or black pepper

1 pound boneless steak, such as flank, hanger, strip, rib eye, or flap

Northeastern Thai Dipping Sauce (page 238), for serving

Jasmine Rice (page 53), for serving

Optional garnish: sliced shallots, diced tomato, fresh mint

1. In a small bowl, mix the soy sauce, garlic, fish sauce, sugar, and pepper until the sugar is dissolved. Transfer the marinade to a shallow bowl, baking dish, or a resealable plastic bag.

2. Submerge the steaks in the marinade, and place in the refrigerator to marinate for a minimum of 30 minutes (and up to 1 hour).

3. Cook the steaks on a charcoal or gas grill on high, or on an oiled stovetop grill pan over medium-heat heat, to medium-rare, about 140°F on an instant-read meat thermometer, 5 to 10 minutes, depending on thickness of steak and cooking method.

*continued*

4. Remove from the heat, cover with aluminum foil, and let rest for 5 to 10 minutes.

5. Slice the meat against the grain into thick strips, and serve with the dipping sauce and rice.

**Serving Suggestion:** Serve together with sliced cucumber, tomato wedges, and lettuce leaves.

**Leftover Tip:** Use any leftover grilled steak to make Grilled Steak Salad (page 114).

# SPICY STIR-FRIED BEEF WITH MUSHROOMS

*Nuea Pad Prik Sod*

SPICE LEVEL: MILD

PREP TIME: 10 MINUTES, PLUS 5 MINUTES TO REST · COOK TIME: 10 MINUTES

NUT-FREE

This recipe (as well as the Stir-Fried Beef with Broccoli recipe, page 209) borrows the Chinese cooking technique "velveting" (page 204), in which the meat is briefly marinated before cooking to make it tender and silky. Velveting can be used in any stir-fry recipe calling for small pieces of meat. For heat, you can adjust the number and type of chiles, to your taste, or seed them for a milder dish; it's nice to use a mix of green and red peppers for aesthetics as well as a balance of heat and flavor. SERVES 4

¼ cup plus 2 tablespoons water, divided

½ teaspoon baking soda

1 pound boneless beef (such as flank steak), cut against the grain into ½-inch by 2- to 3-inch slices

2 teaspoons cornstarch

2 tablespoons vegetable oil

1 tablespoon minced garlic
(2 large cloves)

1 small onion, cut into ½-inch wedges

1 cup sliced mushrooms

2 fresh green Thai bird's-eye, jalapeño, or serrano chiles, stemmed and quartered lengthwise

2 fresh red Thai bird's-eye, jalapeño, or serrano chiles, stemmed and quartered lengthwise

2 tablespoons oyster sauce

Jasmine Rice (page 53), for serving

1. In a medium bowl, mix 2 tablespoons of the water with the baking soda. Add the beef, and toss to coat. Set aside for at least 5 minutes (and up to 15 minutes) to tenderize.

2. Meanwhile, in a small bowl, whisk the ¼ cup water and the cornstarch, and set aside.

3. When the beef is done tenderizing, rinse it well under running water, and drain well.

*continued*

4. In a large wok or skillet, heat the oil. Add the garlic, and stir-fry until fragrant and light golden, about 30 seconds.

5. Add the beef, and stir-fry until just browned, 2 to 3 minutes.

6. Add the onion, and stir-fry until crisp-tender, 3 to 4 minutes.

7. Add the mushrooms and green and red chiles, and stir-fry until the mushrooms are softened, about 2 minutes.

8. Add the oyster sauce and the cornstarch-water mixture, and stir until the sauce is thickened, about 30 seconds.

9. Serve immediately with Jasmine Rice.

**Simple Swaps:** *You can use any type of fresh or dried mushroom in this dish. If using dried mushrooms, soak them in warm water for 10 to 20 minutes before using, to soften.*

# STIR-FRIED BEEF WITH BROCCOLI

### Pad Nuea Gup Broccoli

SPICE LEVEL: NONE

PREP TIME: 5 MINUTES · COOK TIME: 10 MINUTES

NUT-FREE

A quick-and-easy mild stir-fry that will please even the pickiest eaters, this dish is quite similar to the gravy poured on top of stir-fried rice noodles to make Rad Na (page 78). In Thailand, it is made with Chinese broccoli (also known as *gai lan*); feel free to use that, broccoli rabe, or broccolini instead of the broccoli florets. If you want to spice it up a bit, you can add 1 or 2 red bird's-eye, jalapeño, or serrano chiles (stemmed and sliced lengthwise) at the same time as the broccoli. **SERVES 4**

4 tablespoons water, divided

½ teaspoon baking soda

1 pound boneless beef (such as flank steak), cut against the grain into ½-inch by 2- to 3-inch slices

1 pound broccoli

1 teaspoon cornstarch

2 tablespoons vegetable oil

1 tablespoon minced garlic (2 large cloves)

2 tablespoons oyster sauce

1 tablespoon soy sauce

1. In a medium bowl, mix 2 tablespoons of the water and the baking soda. Add the beef, and toss to coat. Set aside for at least 5 minutes (and up to 15) to tenderize.

2. Meanwhile, cut the broccoli florets into 2-inch pieces. Peel the stems, and cut crosswise into thin slices.

3. Bring a large pot of water to boil over high heat. Plunge the broccoli (florets and stems) into the water, and blanch just until bright green and crisp-tender, 1 to 1½ minutes. Rinse under cold running water, drain well, and set aside.

4. When the beef is done tenderizing, rinse it well under running water, and drain well.

5. In a small bowl, whisk together the remaining 2 tablespoons of water and the cornstarch, and set aside.

*continued*

6. In a large wok or skillet over medium heat, heat the oil. Add the garlic, and stir-fry until light golden and fragrant, 30 seconds to 1 minute.

7. Add the beef, and stir-fry until no longer pink, 3 to 4 minutes.

8. Add the broccoli, the remaining 1 cup water, oyster sauce, and soy sauce; raise the heat to high; and bring to a boil.

9. Give the cornstarch mixture a stir, add it to the wok, and simmer until the sauce thickens, about 2 minutes. Serve immediately.

**Serving Suggestion:** *Serve sprinkled with a pinch of ground white pepper, or with Spicy Fish Sauce (page 233) or Pickled Chiles in Vinegar (page 231).*

**Variations:** *Optional additions include fresh or canned baby corn, mushrooms, and water chestnuts.*

# SWEET-AND-SOUR PORK

*Moo Priew Wan*

SPICE LEVEL: NONE

PREP TIME: 10 MINUTES · COOK TIME: 10 MINUTES

GLUTEN-FREE · SOY-FREE · NUT-FREE

This Thai-style version of the famous Chinese dish is much lighter and fresher—no deep-fried batter, red food coloring, ketchup, or gloopy sauce in sight. If you're not a fan of Chinese-American takeout-joint versions, give this one a try—I think you'll be pleasantly surprised. It can also be made with chicken or shrimp. **SERVES 4**

2 tablespoons vegetable oil

1 tablespoon minced garlic
(2 large cloves)

1 pound boneless pork, cut against the grain into bite-size chunks about ½ inch wide and 2 to 3 inches long

1 small onion, cut in 1-inch wedges

2 small Persian cucumbers or 1 large English cucumber, quartered lengthwise and cut into 1½-inch chunks

2 large tomatoes, cored and cut into 8 wedges

1 cup 1-inch chunks pineapple (optional)

2 scallions, cut into 2-inch lengths, white parts also halved lengthwise

3 tablespoons fish sauce

2 tablespoons water

4 teaspoons palm sugar or granulated sugar

4 teaspoons distilled white vinegar

Jasmine Rice (page 53), for serving

1. In a large wok (don't use a new wok or the vinegar can strip the seasoning) or skillet over medium heat, heat the oil. Add the garlic, and stir-fry until just lightly colored, 20 to 30 seconds.

2. Add the pork, and stir-fry until browned, about 2 minutes.

3. Add the onion, and stir-fry until crisp-tender, 3 to 4 minutes.

4. Add the cucumber, tomatoes, pineapple (if using), and scallions, and stir-fry until the tomatoes and scallions are slightly softened and the cucumbers are crisp-tender, 2 to 3 minutes more.

5. Add the fish sauce, water, sugar, and vinegar, and stir well until the sugar is dissolved. Adjust the seasoning to taste, as necessary, and serve immediately with Jasmine Rice.

# CRISPY GARLIC-PEPPER PORK

## *Moo Gratiem Prik Thai*

SPICE LEVEL: MILD

PREP TIME: 10 MINUTES, PLUS 30 MINUTES TO MARINATE · COOK TIME: 5 MINUTES

NUT-FREE

This delicious, crisp-fried pork is a classic recipe that uses pepper for heat instead of chiles. This intensely flavored, garlicky dish is often eaten for breakfast in Thailand, together with white rice, Sticky Rice (page 55), or Rice Porridge (page 62). You can also serve it as an appetizer or as part of a larger meal. SERVES 4

1 tablespoon coriander seed or 4 teaspoons ground coriander

1 tablespoon white or black peppercorns or 4 teaspoons ground white or black pepper

2 tablespoons chopped garlic (3 or 4 large cloves)

Vegetable oil, if needed for blending

1 tablespoon fish sauce

1 tablespoon soy sauce

1 teaspoon palm sugar, light brown sugar, or granulated sugar

1 pound boneless pork chops or pork loin, cut against the grain into ¼-inch-thick, 1- to 2-inch-long, 1-inch-wide slices

Neutral oil for frying, such as peanut or refined coconut oil

1.  In a small, dry skillet over medium-low heat, toast the coriander seed until fragrant, about 1 minute. Remove from the heat and let cool.

2.  In a mortar and pestle or spice grinder, grind the coriander seed and peppercorns to form a coarse powder.

3.  In the mortar and pestle or in a blender or food processor, pound or blend the garlic with the coriander and peppercorns to form a coarse paste. (If necessary, you can add a bit of vegetable oil to the blender or food processor to aid in blending.)

4.  Transfer the paste to a medium bowl, and stir in the fish sauce, soy sauce, and sugar.

5. Add the sliced pork, and toss to coat the pieces evenly. Transfer to the refrigerator to marinate for at least 30 minutes or up to 1 hour.

6. In a wok or skillet over medium heat, heat about ½ inch of oil until shimmering.

7. Fry the pork until crisp, browned, and cooked through, 3 to 4 minutes. Stir with wooden or bamboo chopsticks or tongs, and adjust the heat, as necessary, to avoid burning the garlic. Serve immediately.

**Ingredient Tip:** *It's best to use whole coriander and peppercorns, rather than ground, since whole spices have much more flavor, but if you can't find them, you can use ground coriander and pepper.*

**Serving Suggestion:** *Serve with Jasmine Rice (page 53) or Sticky Rice (page 55), cucumber slices, and Chiles in Lime Sauce (page 232). For extra garlicky flavor, top with Fried Garlic (page 234).*

**Simple Swaps:** *You can also use white- or dark-meat chicken, or any other meat, in this recipe.*

# GRILLED PORK SKEWERS

*Moo Ping*

SPICE LEVEL: NONE

PREP TIME: 5 MINUTES, PLUS 30 MINUTES TO MARINATE
AND SOAK · COOK TIME: 10 MINUTES

NUT-FREE

This is one of the most popular street foods in Thailand (just one taste and you'll see why), and many people eat these as an on-the-go afternoon snack or even for break-fast, together with Sticky Rice (page 55). You can serve these with Northeastern Thai Dipping Sauce for Grilled Meats (page 238) if you want to add some tangy spice, but they're plenty flavorful enough on their own. The sugar caramelizes as they cook, and the coconut milk keeps them tender and juicy. This recipe uses an abbreviated marinating time in the interest of convenience, but the results are still incredible; if you have the time, you can marinate the meat for 2 hours and up to overnight. **MAKES ABOUT 15 TO 20 SKEWERS**

2 tablespoons finely chopped garlic (3 or 4 large cloves)

1 tablespoon finely chopped cilantro root or stem

½ teaspoon white or black peppercorns

3 tablespoons grated palm sugar or light brown sugar

2 tablespoons water

2 tablespoons black soy sauce (aka "dark soy sauce"; see page 8)

1 tablespoon oyster sauce

2 teaspoons fish sauce

1 pound pork shoulder, cut against the grain into bite-size pieces (about ½ inch by 2 inches)

¼ cup coconut milk

1. In a mortar and pestle or in a blender or food processor, pound or blend the garlic, cilantro roots or stems, and peppercorns to form a fine paste. Transfer to a medium bowl, stir in the sugar, water, soy sauce, oyster sauce, and fish sauce, and stir until the sugar is dissolved.

2. Add the pork, and toss to coat evenly. Refrigerate for at least 30 minutes (and up to overnight) to marinate.

3. Meanwhile, soak 20 bamboo skewers in cold water for 30 minutes (this helps prevent them from burning during cooking).

4. Thread the marinated pork pieces onto the skewers, stacking a few pieces on each skewer to fill about half of the skewer. I generally put about 4 or 5 pieces on each skewer.

5. Brush the meat lightly with coconut milk.

6. Cook on an oiled gas grill, charcoal grill, or stovetop grill pan over medium-high heat, turning to cook both sides evenly and basting occasionally with additional coconut milk, as needed, until cooked through and slightly charred on the outside, 8 to 10 minutes, and serve.

**Simple Swaps:** These are typically made with pork, but you can also use beef, chicken, or any other protein.

# CHAPTER TEN

# Drinks and Desserts

Drinks are important in a country as hot as Thailand, and some favorite beverages have become wildly popular abroad. In this chapter, Thai-Style Limeade and Thai Iced Tea are presented in traditional versions along with suggestions for some unusual modern variations.

Though there is a vast and rich repertoire of Thai desserts, few ever appear on Thai restaurant menus abroad. I don't know if that's because many are elaborate and time-consuming to make, or because restaurateurs assume (perhaps rightly) that they might be too bizarre for Western tastes.

Most Thai desserts are far less sweet than their Western counterparts, and they often feature sweet-and-savory flavor combos that can seem strange or downright off-putting to the unaccustomed palate. *Khanom krok*, for example, one of my favorites, are little cup-shaped coconut puddings often topped with scallions, corn, or even dried shrimp.

Rather than as a final course, sweets are eaten throughout the day in Thailand—even for breakfast! Most often, an assortment of cut fresh fruit or fruit in iced syrup is served to close out a meal.

# Pairing Drinks with Thai Food

Historically, Thais didn't drink anything besides water or hot tea with meals.

But for those who enjoy an alcoholic beverage with a meal, a light, slightly sweet beer always goes well with Thai food. Well-known Thai brands include Singha (pronounced "sing") and Chang. Citrusy Belgian-style white beers are also a good choice.

For those who prefer wine, pairing with Thai food can be tricky. The fact that lots of dishes with strong flavors and very different flavor profiles are usually eaten together in a single meal makes it particularly challenging. As a rule of thumb, avoid any oaky or tannic wines with Thai food—the wine will ruin the taste of the food and vice versa.

Off-dry, acidic, floral, or fruity white wines, particularly those from Germany, Austria, or Alsace, such as Riesling and Gewürztraminer, are generally a safe bet. Pinot Gris from Alsace works particularly well, as do Sancerre, Chenin blanc, Sémillon, and Viognier. I've also found that dry rosés and sparkling whites, such as Prosecco or a slightly sweet Champagne (such as Pol Roger) are a good match.

Reds are notoriously hard to pair with Thai food, but there are a few dishes, such as Mussamun Curry (page 154), that could go well with a fruity, acidic red such as a light Shiraz or Beaujolais. Lambrusco, a sparkling red from Italy, would also work well with many Thai dishes.

As a plus, the alcohol in beer or wine helps tame the heat of any particularly spicy dish (as does milk, so Thai Iced Tea (page 220) can play the same spice-antidote role for children or nondrinkers).

# THAI-STYLE LIMEADE

## Nam Manow

PREP TIME: 5 MINUTES

GLUTEN-FREE · SOY-FREE · NUT-FREE · VEGAN

This tangy, refreshing drink is a wonderful thirst-quencher for sultry summer days. It's less sweet than Western versions, with a pinch of salt to round out the taste. Typically, it contains a bit of the lime pulp as well as the juice. Starting off with a bit of boiling water helps avoid gritty, undissolved sugar in the limeade, without the need to prepare a separate simple syrup. **SERVES 1**

2 tablespoons boiling water

4 teaspoons granulated sugar
(or to taste)

Pinch salt

4 tablespoons freshly squeezed lime juice
(or to taste)

¾ cup chilled water

Ice

1. In a tall glass, pour the boiling water over the sugar and salt. Stir well until the sugar dissolves completely.

2. Stir in the lime juice and the chilled water, and add ice. Stir a few times to chill the drink quickly; adjust the sweetness to your taste, as necessary; and serve.

**Variations:** For jasmine or pandan limeade: *Add 1 drop of jasmine or pandan flavoring (available in Southeast Asian markets).* For basil-limeade, mint-limeade, ginger-limeade, or lemongrass-limeade: *Muddle the sugar syrup with 4 leaves of chopped fresh mint or Thai sweet basil, 1 thin slice of bruised ginger, or 1 tablespoon roughly chopped lemongrass, and then strain out after adding water and lime juice.* For sparkling limeade: *Mix the simple syrup with chilled sparkling water or soda water in place of the chilled water.*

# THAI ICED TEA

## Cha Yen

PREP TIME: 5 MINUTES, PLUS 10 MINUTES TO STEEP

GLUTEN-FREE · SOY-FREE · NUT-FREE · VEGETARIAN

When I was little, one of my Thai restaurant rituals was ordering this strong brew of sweet, cool, creamy, sunset-orange tea swirling into billows of white milk. The smoky tea leaves are perfumed with cinnamon, star anise, and vanilla, with coloring added for that brilliant hue. It's typically made with both sweetened condensed milk and evaporated milk, which can be a bit cloying. The great thing about making your own is that you can control the sweetness and use lighter or nondairy alternatives. **SERVES 4**

½ cup Thai tea (see Ingredient Tip)

4 cups water

½ cup granulated sugar (or to taste)

Ice

1 cup (or to taste) half-and-half, evaporated milk, milk, light cream, coconut milk, soy milk, or almond milk, divided

1. Put the tea in a large, heat-proof pitcher, bowl, or saucepan.

2. In a medium saucepan over high heat, bring the water to a boil.

3. Pour the boiling water over the tea, stir in the sugar until dissolved, and let steep for 5 to 10 minutes, to your desired strength.

4. Strain through a very fine mesh metal strainer or coffee filter.

5. Divide the tea evenly among 4 tall glasses, add ice, and pour 3 to 4 tablespoons of your choice of milk, cream, or nondairy options over each serving.

**Variations:** For Thai Lime Tea: *Instead of milk, add a bit of freshly squeezed lime juice to hot or iced Thai Tea.* For Thai Iced Bubble Tea: *Simmer ½ cup dried boba tapioca pearls (sold in Asian markets or online) in 4 cups water until tender, 20 to 25 minutes; remove from the heat and let sit, covered, for another 20 minutes, and then rinse, drain, let cool, and add to the tea.*

# TROPICAL FRUIT COCKTAIL WITH CRUSHED ICE

## Polamai Loy Gaew

PREP TIME: 5 MINUTES

GLUTEN-FREE · SOY-FREE · NUT-FREE · VEGAN

This is a supremely simple and elegant dessert, refreshing on a hot day or after a heavy meal. I debated whether to include it, since it's so basic, but it's one of the few desserts you'll often find in a US Thai restaurant, and it was a staple in our house when I was growing up. You can use just one fruit or a mixture. Sometimes the syrup is infused with spices or flowers, but my mother always served it quite simply. I especially love palm seeds (*look chit*), also known as "sugar palm nuts" or "kaong," jelly-like on the outside and a bit crunchy inside. **SERVES 4**

2 cans tropical fruit in syrup (options include: rambutan stuffed with pineapple, lychee, jackfruit, longan, sliced toddy palm seed, young coconut, mandarin oranges, or mixed tropical fruit cocktail)

½ cup nata de coco (a firm jelly made from coconut) or palm seeds (optional)

Crushed ice

1. In a medium bowl, mix the undrained cans of fruit, and stir in the drained nata de coco or palm seeds (if using).

2. Distribute evenly, including some syrup, among 4 small serving bowls.

3. Add crushed ice to each bowl, and serve.

**Variations:** *For a fancier version, you can use fresh tropical fruit, stir ¼ to ½ cup coconut milk or coconut cream into the syrup, or add just a few drops of jasmine or pandan flavoring (available in Southeast Asian markets) to the syrup.*

# BANANAS IN COCONUT MILK

## Gluay Buat Chi

PREP TIME: 5 MINUTES · COOK TIME: 5 MINUTES

GLUTEN-FREE · SOY-FREE · NUT-FREE · VEGAN

This is a quick and simple yet comforting dessert. The poetic Thai name means "bananas entering nunhood," some say because the bananas enveloped in warm, sweet coconut milk recall the white robes (and perhaps also the shaved heads) of Buddhist nuns. There are many different types of banana in Thailand, and this dessert is typically made with just-ripe *nam wah* bananas, a short, sturdy, bulbous type, analogous to Burro (also known as Chunky) bananas. You can often find them in Asian and Latin American grocery stores, but if not, any other small banana is a good second choice. Otherwise, the ubiquitous Cavendish banana also works. SERVES 4

8 small, just-ripe Burro, red, Manzano, baby, or finger bananas or 4 large, just-ripe Cavendish bananas

4 cups coconut milk

¼ cup granulated sugar

Pinch salt

1. If using small bananas, peel them, halve them lengthwise, and then halve them crosswise, yielding approximately 2-inch lengths. If using large bananas, peel them, halve them lengthwise, and then cut each half into 2-inch chunks.

2. In a medium saucepan over medium-low heat, bring the coconut milk, sugar, and salt to a simmer.

3. Add the bananas, and cook just until heated through, 2 to 3 minutes. The bananas should be a bit soft, but not mushy. Cavendish bananas will cook and soften faster than sturdier bananas.

4. Distribute among 4 small bowls and serve.

**Variations:** *The same dessert can be made with small chunks of kabocha squash, pumpkin, taro, or sweet potato (these will take longer to cook, 5 to 10 minutes).*

# MANGO WITH SWEET COCONUT STICKY RICE

*Khao Niew Mamuang*

PREP TIME: 10 MINUTES PLUS, 2 HOURS TO SOAK · COOK TIME: 30 MINUTES

GLUTEN-FREE · SOY-FREE · NUT-FREE · VEGAN

This is the probably the best-known Thai dessert, and with good reason: Something about the interplay of cool, sweet mango, creamy coconut milk, and warm, chewy sticky rice is infinitely satisfying. A friend served this at her wedding in lieu of wedding cake, and I was delighted! A perfectly ripe, good-quality mango is essential for this dish; look for long, thin, yellow-skinned Ataúlfo (also called Champagne or honey) mangos, which are smooth, velvety, and flavorful. Traditionally the sticky rice is cooked in a special urn-shaped pot and cone-shaped bamboo steamer, but you can use any of the methods described below. **SERVES 4**

1 cup Thai sticky (glutinous) rice (see page 55)

⅔ cup coconut milk

¼ cup granulated sugar

¼ teaspoon salt

4 ripe Ataúlfo mangos

Toasted sesame seeds, for garnish (optional)

1. In a medium bowl, place the rice in enough warm water to cover, and soak for at least 2 hours and up to overnight.

2. When ready to proceed, in a small saucepan over medium heat, heat the coconut milk, sugar, and salt, stirring constantly with a wooden spoon, until the sugar has dissolved completely. Remove from the heat and set aside.

3. Rinse the soaked rice gently several times until the water runs clear. You can do this by adding cold water to the rice, swishing it around with your fingers, and then gently pouring off the water into a sink, being careful not to lose any grains down the drain in the process.

4. In a steamer or large pot over high heat, bring 2 inches of water to a boil.

*continued*

5. To steam the rice, use either a fine-mesh strainer (with a lip or hook that supports it on the edge of a pot), a mesh splatter guard, or a stacking bamboo or metal steamer. If using a strainer, place the drained, soaked rice in the strainer over the boiling water and cover. If using a splatter guard, place the guard on top of the pot and arrange the drained, soaked rice in an even mound in the center of the guard; cover with a domed pot lid or inverted stainless-steel bowl. If using a steamer, line the steamer with a piece of cheesecloth or muslin and place the rice in the center in a small, even mound, about 1 to 2 inches thick. Fold the edges of the cloth up around the mound to wrap it, and cover the steamer with a lid.

6. Adjust the heat so that the water is at a steady but gentle boil, and steam until the rice is softened, translucent, and sticks together in lumps when pressed, 20 to 30 minutes.

7. Transfer the rice to the saucepan containing the sweetened coconut milk, stir a few times so that it's evenly submerged in the milk, cover, and let sit for at least 30 minutes to absorb the coconut milk.

8. Meanwhile, prepare the mangos: Peel them using a sharp paring knife, and then carefully extract each half of the mango, sliding the blade of the knife right next to the flat side of the seed on each side. Cut each half crosswise into 1-inch slices, and arrange on a plate with a mound of sticky rice.

9. Sprinkle with sesame seeds (if using) and serve.

# FRIED BANANAS

## *Gluay Khaek*

PREP TIME: 5 MINUTES · COOK TIME: ABOUT 25 MINUTES

GLUTEN-FREE · SOY-FREE · NUT-FREE · VEGAN

This is perhaps the second-most-famous Thai dessert after mangos and sticky rice. This recipe makes fried bananas as they're sold on the street in Thailand: thin strips in a crisp, golden-brown batter flecked with sesame seeds. Thai restaurants abroad often use long Cavendish bananas, the most common cultivar, but Thai street vendors use short, firm *nam wah* bananas, whose counterpart is the Burro (or Chunky) banana. Regular Cavendish bananas tend to turn mushy when cooked this way, but if that's all you can find, be sure to choose firm ones that are still a bit green.

**SERVES 4 TO 6**

6 slightly underripe Burro or red bananas or 3 underripe Cavendish bananas

1 cup rice flour

½ cup unsweetened shredded coconut

¼ cup sugar

1 tablespoon toasted sesame seeds

1½ teaspoons baking soda

½ teaspoon salt

¾ cup water

Neutral vegetable oil, for frying

1.  Peel the bananas and cut lengthwise into 4 slices about ¼ inch thick. (If using long Cavendish bananas, halve each one lengthwise and crosswise to form four 3-inch chunks).

2.  In a large mixing bowl, whisk together the rice flour, coconut, sugar, sesame seeds, baking soda, and salt.

3.  Whisk the water in gradually to form a batter. (The batter will not be very thick; the bananas should still be slightly visible when battered.) Set aside.

4.  In a large sauté pan, wok, Dutch oven, or deep fryer over high heat, heat about 1½ inches of oil to 360°F. (The temperature will drop when you add the bananas.)

*continued*

5. Dip the banana slices or chunks in the batter, drop each piece quickly into the oil (fry 4 to 5 pieces at a time; don't overcrowd the pot), and fry until crisp and a rich golden brown, 2 to 3 minutes. Regulate the heat as necessary to maintain the temperature at a steady 350°F while frying; a deep-fat frying thermometer that clips to the side of the pot is helpful for this. Use wooden chopsticks or tongs to turn the pieces as they cook so that they brown evenly.

6. Remove the fried bananas with a mesh skimmer or slotted metal spoon, and drain well on a paper towel–lined plate. Serve hot.

**Ingredient Tip:** You can find rice flour in Asian markets, health food stores, or online. You can substitute regular all-purpose flour for the rice flour, but your batter will be heavier and crunchier.

**Simple Swaps:** Street vendors who sell these often also sell ¼-inch-thick slices of sweet potato fried in the same batter–give it a try! They will cook in the same amount of time and can be fried together with the bananas.

# BAKED SWEET POTATO-COCONUT CUSTARD

## Khanom Mo Gaeng Mun Tet

PREP TIME: 5 MINUTES · COOK TIME: 45 MINUTES

GLUTEN-FREE · SOY-FREE · NUT-FREE · VEGETARIAN

This dish is typically topped with fried shallots, but if that's too weird, you can sprinkle it with toasted, shredded coconut before serving or leave it plain. It tastes great chilled and can be stored in the refrigerator, wrapped in plastic wrap, for several days. You can use pumpkin or kabocha squash in place of the sweet potato. MAKES 12 TO 16 SQUARES

5 large eggs

¾ cup palm sugar or light brown sugar

1 cup coconut milk

1½ cups cooked, mashed, and cooled sweet potato (see Note)

¼ teaspoon salt

½ cup Crispy Fried Shallots (page 235) or toasted, shredded coconut (see Note on page 125; optional)

1. Preheat the oven to 350°F.

2. In a large mixing bowl, use a wooden spoon or an electric hand mixer to mix the eggs, sugar, coconut milk, sweet potato, and salt until combined.

3. Pour the mixture into a lightly greased, 2-inch-deep, 8-inch-square baking pan (or 11-by-7-by-2-inch rectangular pan), and bake until the top is a deep golden-brown and a toothpick inserted in the center comes out clean, 40 to 45 minutes.

4. Let cool to room temperature, and then sprinkle with the fried shallots or toasted coconut (if using), cut into squares, and serve.

**Note:** *To make the mashed sweet potato, peel and cut 1 pound sweet potatoes into ½-inch slices. Place the potatoes in a large pot with enough water to cover, bring to a boil over high heat, turn the heat to low, and simmer, covered, until tender, 5 to 6 minutes. Drain, mash, and let cool.*

# CHAPTER ELEVEN

# Sauces and Condiments

There are countless Thai chili sauces (nam prik), dipping sauces (nam jim), and other condiments, including regional variations. Here we have just a few of the most common and versatile ones. With any of the uncooked sauces, you can use all red chiles, all green, or a mixture of the two (my personal preference, both for aesthetic sense and a more well-balanced flavor). Roasted Chili Paste (page 240) and Satay Peanut Sauce (page 243), when paired with toast, crackers, crispy pork rinds (cracklings), shrimp chips, or crisp raw vegetables, make a quick and simple appetizer or snack and are great finger foods for parties. And these sauces are not just great with Thai food—try them with any of your favorite dishes!

# GROUND ROASTED CHILI POWDER

## Prik Pohn Kua

PREP TIME: 5 MINUTES · COOK TIME: 5 MINUTES

GLUTEN-FREE · SOY-FREE · NUT-FREE · VEGAN

One of the most basic Thai condiments, this chili powder is available in most homes or street-food stalls to adjust spiciness to individual tastes. Gently toasting dried red chiles gives them a wonderful warm, fruity aroma and a rich, nutty flavor. This is an ingredient in many of the salads in chapter 4 but can be used for amping up flavor in any dish. This recipe makes a relatively mild version. For a spicier powder, leave the seeds in, or use dried Thai bird's-eye chiles, piri piri peppers, or cayenne peppers together with (or instead of) the long chiles. MAKES ABOUT ¼ CUP

20 dried red Thai long chiles
(2 to 3 inches long), stemmed
and seeded

1. In a dry skillet over medium heat, toast the chiles, shaking the skillet constantly to prevent scorching, until fragrant and darkened (but not blackened), 1 to 2 minutes.

2. Remove from the heat, and let cool completely.

3. In a granite mortar and pestle or a spice grinder, grind the chiles to form a coarse powder. (How coarse or fine you make the powder is up to you, but I prefer it with some flakes remaining.)

4. Store in an airtight glass jar in a cool, dark, dry place for up to 1 month.

**Note:** *To stem and seed dried chiles, simply use your fingers to snap off the stem and discard it. Then squeeze each chile gently, and it should simply break open. Shake it to remove the seeds inside; they should simply fall out. Wear disposable rubber gloves for this operation to prevent "chile hands."*

# PICKLED CHILES IN VINEGAR

## Prik Dong

SPICE LEVEL: HOT

PREP TIME: 5 MINUTES, PLUS AT LEAST 15 MINUTES TO SIT

GLUTEN-FREE · SOY-FREE · NUT-FREE · VEGAN

This super-simple sauce is a traditional accompaniment to noodle dishes such as Rad Na (page 78) and Pad See Ew (page 75), as well as an all-purpose condiment that adds crunch, spiciness, and bright sourness to just about any Thai dish. In Thailand, it's typically present in the seasoning caddies of casual restaurants and sidewalk food stalls along with ground red chiles, white sugar, and fish sauces (spicy or plain). The caddy is the equivalent of the salt and pepper shakers in Western restaurants—they allow a diner to adjust and balance each dish's flavor to their liking.

**MAKES ABOUT 1¼ CUPS**

6 or 7 red Thai long chiles (see page 10), stemmed

6 or 7 green Thai long chiles, stemmed

1 cup distilled white vinegar

1. Cut the chiles crosswise into thin rings, about ⅛ inch.

2. In a medium bowl, mix the chiles into the vinegar.

3. Let sit for at least 15 minutes, or, ideally, 1 to 2 days, to let the chiles pickle and mellow and the flavors develop.

4. Serve in a small bowl with a small spoon for diners to dose it out over their individual servings as desired. It will keep for up to 3 days at room temperature or up to 2 weeks refrigerated in a small sealed glass jar. The longer it sits, the milder it will be, and the chiles will soften over time.

**Dial Up (or Down) the Heat:** *Use 10 to 12 red and 10 to 12 green bird's-eye chiles in place of the long chiles for a spicier sauce; use 12 serranos or jalapeños for a milder one. For any of these chiles, removing the seeds will tone down the heat.*

# CHILES IN LIME SAUCE

## *Prik Manow*

SPICE LEVEL: HOT

PREP TIME: 5 MINUTES

GLUTEN-FREE · SOY-FREE · NUT-FREE

Similar to Pickled Chiles in Vinegar (page 231), this is an all-purpose condiment used for adjusting the spice, salt, and sourness in just about any dish to each diner's personal taste. The difference is that this needs to be made and used right away; it doesn't keep well because lime juice loses its bright freshness quickly. Other than that, they are interchangeable in their usage. **MAKES ABOUT ¼ CUP**

4 fresh red Thai bird's-eye, jalapeño, or serrano chiles, stemmed

¼ cup plus 2 tablespoons freshly squeezed lime juice

3 tablespoons fish sauce

1. Cut the chiles crosswise into ¼-inch rings. (Seed the chiles before slicing for a milder sauce.)

2. In a small bowl, mix the lime juice, fish sauce, and chopped chiles, and serve.

# SPICY FISH SAUCE

## Nam Pla Prik

SPICE LEVEL: HOT

PREP TIME: 5 MINUTES

GLUTEN-FREE · SOY-FREE · NUT-FREE

Another uber-simple, all-purpose sauce that can be used to add salt and spice to most Thai dishes, particularly rice dishes, nam pla prik is usually served in a little dish next to the ubiquitous condiment caddy found at casual Thai restaurants, and with most homemade Thai meals as well. This is the most basic version–some include thinly sliced garlic or shallots. Feel free to customize it to your own taste.

**MAKES ABOUT ¼ CUP**

2 red Thai bird's-eye chiles, stemmed

2 green Thai bird's-eye chiles, stemmed

½ cup fish sauce

1. Cut the chiles crosswise into thin rings, about ⅛ inch.

2. In a small bowl, mix the chiles into the fish sauce.

3. Serve in a small, shallow bowl with a small spoon. The sauce is best made fresh but can be refrigerated in a sealed jar for up to 2 weeks.

# FRIED GARLIC IN OIL

### Nam Mun Gratiem Jiew

SPICE LEVEL: NONE

PREP TIME: 5 MINUTES · COOK TIME: 5 MINUTES

GLUTEN-FREE · SOY-FREE · NUT-FREE · VEGAN

This is an incredibly versatile and simple condiment. You can buy fried garlic and fried shallots in Asian markets to use as toppings on noodle soups and Quick Congee Rice Porridge (page 62), for dipping dumplings, or seasoning any dish you desire, but the taste can't compare to homemade, and the oil the garlic is fried in can also be used, with or without the fried garlic bits, as a flavor enhancer on all kinds of dishes.

**MAKES ABOUT 1 CUP**

4 large garlic cloves, finely and evenly minced

1 cup vegetable oil

1. In a small saucepan over medium-low heat, cook the garlic in the oil, stirring frequently with a wooden spoon, until the garlic turns a light, golden straw color, about 2 minutes.

2. Remove the saucepan from the heat, and let sit for about 10 to 15 seconds. The garlic will continue to cook in the oil and turn crisp and a rich golden color (be careful not to overcook the garlic or it will taste bitter). Pour the garlic and oil carefully into a clean, dry glass jar; let cool completely; and then use immediately or seal and store in a cool, dry place for up to 1 week (do not refrigerate). You can also strain the fried garlic out of the oil and store just the fried garlic, discarding the oil, if you plan to use only the garlic.

**Serving Suggestion:** *My mother, who always had a jar of fried garlic in oil in the cupboard, would sometimes toss it with spaghetti for a sort of Thai-style aglio e olio—a great quick meal or late-night snack that you can make in less than 10 minutes.*

# CRISPY FRIED SHALLOTS

*Hom Jiew*

SPICE LEVEL: NONE

PREP TIME: 5 MINUTES · COOK TIME: 5 MINUTES

GLUTEN-FREE · SOY-FREE · NUT-FREE · VEGAN

Fried garlic's sister condiment, crisp-fried shallots are used as a topping on salads, soups, curries, Rice Porridge (page 62), and many other dishes. They are even used to top some desserts, such as Sweet Potato–Coconut Custard (page 227). You can buy fried shallots in Asian markets, but the taste does not compare to homemade. A mandoline makes slicing the shallots quick and easy and produces even slices that will cook at the same rate. **MAKES ABOUT ½ CUP**

4 shallots, thinly sliced                    ¾ cup vegetable oil

1. In a small saucepan over medium-low heat, cook the shallots in the oil, stirring frequently with a wooden spoon, until the bubbling subsides and the shallots are crisp and light golden brown, 2 to 3 minutes.

2. Strain immediately through a fine-mesh strainer (you can reserve the oil, store it separately, and use it to flavor dishes as well, or you can discard it), and drain the fried shallots on a paper towel–lined plate.

3. When completely cooled, store the fried shallots in an airtight container in a cool, dry place for up to 3 weeks.

# CHILI, GARLIC, AND LIME SAUCE

*Nam Jim Manow*

PREP TIME: 10 MINUTES

GLUTEN-FREE · SOY-FREE · NUT-FREE

This quick, no-cook sauce is wonderful as an accompaniment for grilled, steamed, or fried seafood. In fact, it's often called "Seafood Sauce" because it pairs so well with it. But it's also great on meat dishes, and it always makes an appearance on my family's Thanksgiving table to liven up the turkey. Don't be tempted to omit the sugar; it really pulls all the other flavors together, but the final sauce should not be noticeably sweet.

**MAKES ABOUT ½ CUP**

2 fresh red, green, or a mix of both Thai bird's-eye chiles, stemmed and cut crosswise into thin rings

2 garlic cloves, finely chopped

2 tablespoons fish sauce

7 teaspoons freshly squeezed lime juice

2 teaspoons palm sugar or granulated white sugar

1. In a granite mortar and pestle, pound the chiles and garlic together until they form a coarse paste.

2. Transfer the paste to a small bowl, and stir in the fish sauce.

3. Stir in the lime juice, and mix well.

4. Mix in the sugar, ½ teaspoon at a time, stirring well after each addition, until the sugar is dissolved.

5. The sauce is best served fresh but can be stored in the refrigerator for 1 to 2 days.

**Equipment Tip:** *If you don't have a mortar and pestle, mince the first two ingredients very finely, and then mash them together with the flat side of a chef's knife until a coarse paste forms, or grate the garlic using a Microplane grater, and then mash with the chiles as noted.*

**Recipe Tip:** *Measurements are given as a guideline, since the spiciness of chiles can vary widely, even within the same batch; some brands of fish sauce are far saltier than others; and limes can also vary in sourness, depending on the season and other factors. You can adjust the heat level up or down, depending on your personal taste, using up to 4 or 5 chiles for extra-spicy sauce, or seeding the chiles before use for a milder sauce. Start with the recommended measurement for each ingredient, and then increase the fish sauce, sugar, and lime juice bit by bit (in ¼- or ½-teaspoon increments), tasting as you go along, until you find the harmonious "sweet spot" of balance, when it's not too spicy, not too sour, not too salty, and not too sweet. You will know it when you find it!*

# NORTHEASTERN THAI DIPPING SAUCE FOR GRILLED MEATS

*Nam Jim Jaew*

SPICE LEVEL: MEDIUM

PREP TIME: 5 MINUTES

This nutty, mildly spicy sauce, made with dried red chiles, is a traditional accompaniment for Grilled Chicken (page 45), Grilled Pork (page 214), and Crying Tiger Grilled Steak (page 205) but will go well with any grilled meats. **MAKES ABOUT 1 CUP**

4 teaspoons Ground Roasted Chili Powder (page 230)

⅔ cup fish sauce

Juice of 2 limes

¼ cup thinly sliced shallot

¼ cup very thinly sliced scallion (green parts only)

2 tablespoons chopped fresh cilantro

2 tablespoons tamarind paste (see page 26 or store-bought)

4 teaspoons Roasted Rice Powder (see page 16 or store bought)

3 teaspoons palm sugar or brown sugar

In a small bowl, mix together the chili powder, fish sauce, lime juice, shallot, scallion, cilantro, tamarind paste, rice powder, and sugar until the sugar and tamarind are dissolved. This sauce is best served fresh, but it will keep for up to 1 day in the refrigerator.

# SWEET CHILI SAUCE

*Nam Jim Gai*

SPICE LEVEL: MEDIUM

PREP TIME: 5 MINUTES · COOK TIME: 10 MINUTES

GLUTEN-FREE · SOY-FREE · NUT-FREE · VEGAN

This is the most traditional accompaniment for grilled chicken (page 45). In fact, the name translates as "dipping sauce for chicken." But it's actually a very versatile sauce that can be used as a dipping sauce for many things. You can find it premade in most Asian markets, but it's quick and simple to make your own. This sauce will not be as thick as store-bought, but you can add an additional teaspoon of cornstarch if you prefer it thicker; it will also thicken when refrigerated. **MAKES ABOUT 1 CUP**

4 garlic cloves, chopped

6 fresh red Thai bird's-eye chiles or 3 red jalapeño or serrano chiles, stemmed and chopped

2 dried red chiles (2 to 3 inches long), stemmed and chopped

½ cup distilled white vinegar

¼ cup water

¾ cup granulated sugar

½ teaspoon cornstarch whisked into 1 tablespoon water

1. In a blender or food processor, pulse the garlic, fresh chiles, and dried chiles just until finely chopped.

2. In a small saucepan over medium heat, bring the garlic-chile mixture, vinegar, water, and sugar to a simmer.

3. Simmer, stirring with a wooden spoon, until the sugar dissolves and the sauce thickens slightly, about 8 minutes.

4. Stir in the cornstarch-water mixture, and simmer until it thickens to a syrupy consistency, about 2 minutes longer.

5. Remove from the heat, let cool to room temperature, and serve. It can be refrigerated in a sealed glass jar for several weeks. The sauce will thicken when refrigerated, and the flavor will mellow and grow less spicy over time.

# ROASTED CHILI PASTE

## Nam Prik Pao

SPICE LEVEL: MILD

PREP TIME: 5 MINUTES · COOK TIME: 35 MINUTES

GLUTEN-FREE · SOY-FREE · NUT-FREE

This sweet, oily, smoky paste (sometimes called a "chile jam") has a rich flavor and deep red color from the roasted chiles and spices. It's the key ingredient for Tom Yum Soup (page 93) and in stir-fried dishes such as Spicy Stir-Fried Shrimp with Roasted Chili Paste (page 176). It can be found ready-made in Asian markets (sometimes labeled as "Roasted Red Chili Paste" or "Chili Paste in Soybean Oil"). This recipe makes a relatively mild version. Store-bought versions (often available in mild, medium, and hot) are thicker, spicier, and funkier, since they tend to contain more shrimp paste. **MAKES ABOUT 2 CUPS**

8 dried Thai long, New Mexico, or California chiles

2 tablespoons dried shrimp

⅓ cup plus ¼ cup vegetable oil, divided

⅓ cup very thinly sliced garlic (5 or 6 large cloves)

⅔ cup very thinly sliced shallot (about 2 large shallots)

1 teaspoon shrimp paste

¾ cup palm sugar or light brown sugar, packed

½ cup water

2 tablespoons tamarind paste (see page 26 or store-bought)

2 tablespoons fish sauce

1.  In a dry skillet over medium-low heat, roast the chiles, turning frequently, until fragrant and browned, 1 to 2 minutes. Be careful not to burn them. When roasted, remove them from the heat and transfer them to a shallow bowl. Set aside.

2.  Add the dried shrimp to the dry skillet, and toast until fragrant and lightly browned, 1 to 2 minutes. Transfer them to the same bowl as the chiles.

3.  Add ⅓ cup of the oil to the skillet, and heat over medium heat. When the oil is shimmering hot, add the garlic and fry, stirring frequently to cook evenly and prevent burning, until golden brown, 3 to 4 minutes.

4. Transfer the fried garlic to a shallow bowl using a slotted spoon or mesh skimmer.

5. Add the shallots to the hot oil, lower the heat to medium-low, and fry until golden brown, 4 to 5 minutes.

6. Transfer the fried shallots to the same bowl as the fried garlic.

7. Add the shrimp paste, and fry, stirring, for 1 minute more. (This part will release the full shrimp paste smell—be sure to have your exhaust fan on full power!)

8. Remove from the heat. When all the ingredients have cooled, transfer the chiles, shrimp, fried garlic, fried shallots, and fried shrimp paste together with the frying oil to a blender, and puree to a paste. There should be no chunks left.

9. Add the remaining ¼ cup oil to the skillet, and heat over medium heat.

10. Gently whisk the paste into the oil in the skillet, and then stir in the sugar, water, tamarind paste, and fish sauce.

11. Bring to a simmer, and simmer gently over low heat for 15 to 20 minutes, or until the paste is smooth and has thickened.

12. Remove from the heat, let cool completely, and use immediately or store, refrigerated in a sealed glass jar, for 2 to 3 months, or freeze for up to 6 months. It's normal for oil to separate out, in both homemade and store-bought versions; just stir the oil back in before use.

**Serving Suggestion:** *Spread thinly on toast or crackers for an appetizer or snack, or use in sandwiches or as a dipping sauce for pork rinds or shrimp chips.*

**Equipment Tip:** *A mandoline makes creating paper-thin slices of garlic and shallot for this recipe much easier and faster.*

# CUCUMBER RELISH

## Ajaat

SPICE LEVEL: MEDIUM

PREP TIME: 5 MINUTES · COOK TIME: 5 MINUTES

GLUTEN-FREE · SOY-FREE · NUT-FREE · VEGAN

This sweet-and-tangy refreshing relish is typically eaten with rich dishes as a bright counterpoint. It's traditionally served with grilled Satay Skewers (page 45) and Satay Peanut Sauce (page 243), with Yellow Curry (page 128), and with crisp-fried Fish Cakes (page 41), but you can serve it with any grilled meats, rich curries, or fried starters. It's best made fresh and served immediately, as the cucumbers quickly lose their crispness and start to pickle; they're intended to be eaten when still crunchy.

**MAKES ABOUT 1 CUP**

½ cup thinly sliced cucumber

½ cup distilled white vinegar

¼ cup granulated white sugar

½ teaspoon salt

2 tablespoons very thinly sliced shallot

1 fresh red Thai bird's-eye chile, red jalapeño, or red serrano, stemmed and cut crosswise into ¼-inch slices

1 tablespoon fresh cilantro leaves

1. If using a small cucumber, halve the cucumber lengthwise and then slice into thin half-moons; if using a large cucumber, quarter it lengthwise and cut the quarters into thin triangle-shaped slices.

2. In a small saucepan over medium heat, heat the vinegar, sugar, and salt, stirring with a wooden spoon, just until the sugar dissolves completely. Remove from the heat and let cool to room temperature.

3. In a small bowl, mix to combine the cucumber, shallot, and chile, and pour the cooled vinegar-sugar syrup over.

4. Sprinkle the cilantro leaves on top and serve immediately.

**Ingredient Tip:** *Smaller Persian or pickling cucumbers are best for this recipe, but you can also use a large English cucumber.*

# SATAY PEANUT SAUCE

## Nam Jim Satay

SPICE LEVEL: MILD

PREP TIME: 5 MINUTES · COOK TIME: 5 MINUTES

GLUTEN-FREE · SOY-FREE

This creamy, mildly spicy sauce is the traditional dipping sauce served with Chicken Satay Skewers (page 45), but it can also be used as a topping for steamed or stir-fried vegetables or meat, as a sauce for noodles, in a salad dressing (page 116), and in Pra Ram (page 166). It's traditionally made using ground peanuts, not peanut butter, but my mother used peanut butter, and it's an easy shortcut that doesn't negatively affect the outcome as long as you use natural, unsweetened peanut butter. If you use unsalted peanut butter, increase the amount of fish sauce to taste. MAKES ABOUT 2 CUPS

1 cup coconut milk

1 tablespoon Red Curry Paste (page 130 or store-bought)

1 teaspoon fish sauce

⅓ cup water

1 tablespoon tamarind paste (see page 26 or store-bought), or freshly squeezed lime juice

1 tablespoon palm sugar or brown sugar

½ cup unsweetened natural peanut butter (creamy or chunky)

1. In a medium saucepan, bring all the ingredients to a simmer over medium heat. Reduce the heat to low and simmer gently, stirring occasionally, until the sugar dissolves, the sauce has thickened a bit, and red-orange bubbles of oil start to separate out on top (as with a Thai curry, this sauce traditionally has a little bit of oil on top, but if the oil doesn't separate out, it's not a big deal), about 5 minutes. If it gets too thick, you can thin it with a little more coconut milk or water. Adjust the seasoning to taste with additional fish sauce, tamarind paste, and sugar, as necessary.

2. Remove from the heat and let cool to room temperature before serving. The sauce can be refrigerated for up to 1 week or frozen for several months. It tends to thicken when refrigerated or frozen, so you might need to add a bit of hot water to thin it before use.

# Menus

Aside from one-dish meals like fried-rice, noodle soups, stir-fried noodles, and with-rice dishes such as Stir-Fried Chicken with Basil (page 195), a traditional Thai meal is generally made up of several different dishes (usually anywhere from three to five); served family style, rather than in courses; and all served with a generous amount of Jasmine Rice (page 53) or Sticky Rice (page 55). This type of dish is referred to, in general, as *gup khao* ("with rice"). All dishes are shared by all of the diners, rather than one main dish to each person, as is the custom in many Western-style restaurants.

All of the estimated serving sizes indicated in this book are made with the assumption that the dish will be served together with steamed rice as part of a larger meal. If you want to make one as a one-dish meal to be served on its own, or with only rice, you might need to scale the recipe up. That can be done easily for just about any of the recipes, except for the stir-fried rice and noodle dishes, for reasons explained in the introduction to chapter 3 (page 51).

The concept of balance is important when putting together a Thai menu; for example, a typical Thai meal would not consist of all deep-fried dishes, or only dishes that are very spicy. Aim for a contrast of mild and spicy, sour and sweet, and in textures and temperatures as well–complementing cool or room-temperature plates with some that are steaming hot, or soft or chewy with crispy or crunchy. The balance of flavors is not necessarily achieved within every single dish–though it can be–but within the meal itself, so putting together a successful Thai meal does take a little consideration.

Here are a few suggested menus to get you started:

# QUICK-AND-EASY THAI MENU

Start-to-finish, this menu should take just a little more than 45 minutes. The spicy soup, bright and tangy with fresh lime juice and lemongrass, is balanced by the rich, creamy curry, sweet-tart pineapple, and mild, savory cabbage.

**HOT-AND-SOUR TOM YUM SOUP WITH SHRIMP**
*Tom Yum Goong (page 93)*

**RED CURRY WITH ROAST DUCK AND PINEAPPLE**
*Gaeng Pehd Bped Yang (page 149)*

**STIR-FRIED NAPA CABBAGE**
*Pad Galumplee (page 159)*

**JASMINE RICE**
*Khao Suay (page 53)*

1. Prep all the ingredients for the soup, curry, and stir-fried cabbage (20 minutes).

2. Put the rice on to cook, either on the stovetop or in an electric rice cooker (about 5 minutes).

3. Follow the instructions for the cabbage and set aside, covered, to keep warm (5 minutes).

4. Follow the instructions for the curry recipe through step 4, but don't stir in the basil leaves yet. Cover to keep warm while you make the soup (10 minutes).

5. Follow the instructions for the soup through step 5 (7 minutes).

6. Stir the basil leaves into the curry, sprinkle the cilantro onto the soup, and serve everything together with the rice.

# NORTHEASTERN THAI MENU

These classic dishes from the northeastern Isaan region are often eaten together, and traditionally are eaten with your hands. Diners dip the chicken pieces into the sweet chili sauce and use small balls of sticky rice to pick up pieces of each of the salads. If you soak the sticky rice the night before and use either store-bought or previously made Sweet Chili Sauce, this menu takes about 1 hour to prepare (about 1 hour and 15 minutes with freshly made sauce).

**GRILLED GARLIC-LEMONGRASS CHICKEN**
*Gai Yang (page 200)*

**NORTHEASTERN THAI–STYLE GROUND PORK SALAD**
*Lahb Moo (page 110)*

**GREEN PAPAYA SALAD**
*Som Tum (page 99)*

**SWEET CHILI SAUCE**
*Nam Jim Gai (page 239)*

**STICKY RICE**
*Khao Niew (page 55)*

1. Soak the uncooked glutinous rice for the sticky rice the night before your meal, or at least 4 hours ahead of time.

2. Prep and start marinating the chicken (about 10 minutes).

3. Put the soaked and drained rice on to steam (about 5 minutes).

4. Make the sweet chili sauce or use store-bought sweet chili sauce (about 15 minutes if homemade, can be made up to several weeks ahead of time).

5. Make the ground pork salad and set aside (about 10 minutes).

6. Make the green papaya salad (about 10 minutes).

7. Grill or oven-roast the chicken (about 25 minutes).

# VEGETARIAN THAI MENU

This menu is an example of how easy it is to turn just about any of the recipes in this book into a vegetarian version. If you use store-bought or previously made dipping sauce for the spring rolls, the whole menu should take about 1 hour and 15 minutes (1½ hours with freshly made sauce). To turn this into a vegan Thai menu, replace the Fried Egg Salad with either the Pomelo Salad with Toasted Coconut and Mint (page 108) or the Grilled Eggplant Salad (page 112), seasoning either with salt instead of fish sauce.

**FRESH SPRING ROLLS**
*Poh Piah Sod (page 37)*

**SIMPLE SOUP WITH TOFU, MEATBALLS, AND VEGETABLES**
*Gaeng Jeud Taohu Moo Sup (page 97)*

**FRIED EGG SALAD**
*Yum Kai Dao (page 185)*

**GREEN CURRY WITH PORK, BAMBOO SHOOTS, AND EGGPLANT**
*Gaeng Kiew Wan Moo (page 146)*

**JASMINE RICE**
*Khao Suay (page 53)*

1. Make the spring rolls, omitting the shrimp; cover in plastic wrap and set aside (about 20 minutes).

2. Make the soup, omitting the meatballs and replacing the fish sauce with 1 additional tablespoon soy sauce (about 15 minutes).

3. Put the rice on to cook, either on the stovetop or in an electric rice cooker (about 5 minutes).

4. Make the curry, omitting the pork and seasoning to taste with salt instead of fish sauce (about 20 minutes).

5. Make the salad, seasoning to taste with salt instead of fish sauce (about 15 minutes).

6. Serve the spring rolls as an appetizer or together with the rest of the meal, accompanied by Sweet Chili Sauce (page 239), either homemade (about 15 minutes) or store-bought, topped with a few fresh cilantro leaves and crushed roasted peanuts.

# Measurement Conversions

## VOLUME EQUIVALENTS (LIQUID)

| US STANDARD | US STANDARD (OUNCES) | METRIC (APPROXIMATE) |
|---|---|---|
| 2 tablespoons | 1 fl. oz. | 30 mL |
| ¼ cup | 2 fl. oz. | 60 mL |
| ½ cup | 4 fl. oz. | 120 mL |
| 1 cup | 8 fl. oz. | 240 mL |
| 1½ cups | 12 fl. oz. | 355 mL |
| 2 cups or 1 pint | 16 fl. oz. | 475 mL |
| 4 cups or 1 quart | 32 fl. oz. | 1 L |
| 1 gallon | 128 fl. oz. | 4 L |

## OVEN TEMPERATURES

| FAHRENHEIT (F) | CELSIUS (C) (APPROXIMATE) |
|---|---|
| 250°F | 120°C |
| 300°F | 150°C |
| 325°F | 165°C |
| 350°F | 180°C |
| 375°F | 190°C |
| 400°F | 200°C |
| 425°F | 220°C |
| 450°F | 230°C |

## VOLUME EQUIVALENTS (DRY)

| US STANDARD | METRIC (APPROXIMATE) |
|---|---|
| ⅛ teaspoon | 0.5 mL |
| ¼ teaspoon | 1 mL |
| ½ teaspoon | 2 mL |
| ¾ teaspoon | 4 mL |
| 1 teaspoon | 5 mL |
| 1 tablespoon | 15 mL |
| ¼ cup | 59 mL |
| ⅓ cup | 79 mL |
| ½ cup | 118 mL |
| ⅔ cup | 156 mL |
| ¾ cup | 177 mL |
| 1 cup | 235 mL |
| 2 cups or 1 pint | 475 mL |
| 3 cups | 700 mL |
| 4 cups or 1 quart | 1 L |

## WEIGHT EQUIVALENTS

| US STANDARD | METRIC (APPROXIMATE) |
|---|---|
| ½ ounce | 15 g |
| 1 ounce | 30 g |
| 2 ounces | 60 g |
| 4 ounces | 115 g |
| 8 ounces | 225 g |
| 12 ounces | 340 g |
| 16 ounces or 1 pound | 455 g |

# Resources

## ONLINE RETAILERS

- AMAZON / www.amazon.com
  You can find a variety of nonperishable Asian ingredients via Amazon, as well as Thai and Chinese cookware.

- TEMPLE OF THAI / www.templeofthai.com
  Temple of Thai offers a wide variety of sauces, spices, curry pastes, fresh produce, and other ingredients, as well as granite mortars and pestles, carbon-steel woks, and other cookware.

- GROCERYTHAI / www.grocerythai.com
  This retailer features fresh produce and aromatics as well as canned goods and traditional Thai kitchenware.

- IMPORTFOOD THAI SUPERMARKET / www.importfood.com
  Fresh and nonperishable Thai ingredients, Thai cookware, and traditional Thai ceramics can be sourced here.

# Acknowledgments

I would like to thank my aunt, Sakorn Wheeler, and my cousin, Ornsuang Sutirasakul, for their helpful input and for verifying the accuracy of the Thai characters and transliterations. My heartfelt gratitude goes to my recipe testers, Lauren Buckland Ledbetter, Dan Ratanasit, Michael Wolff, Minu Mohan, and Huan-Hua Chye. Thanks to my sister, Nui, who shares my love of cooking, for reminding me that I was already a cookbook author. Erin Zaleski deserves recognition for her encouragement and for helping me eat vast amounts of Thai food. And I am most grateful to Thomas Moors, who has given unwavering support (and occasional dishwashing assistance) throughout long hours of research, writing, and recipe testing.

# Recipe Index

# Index

CPSIA information can be obtained
at www.ICGtesting.com
Printed in the USA
BVOW11s2116270917
495820BV00002B/2/P